JOURNALS

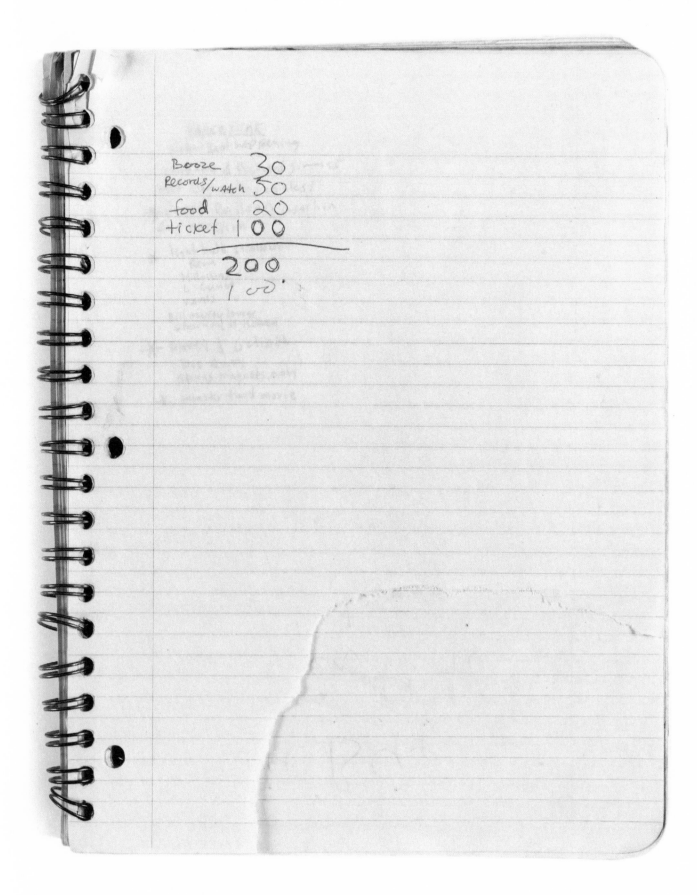

Booze   30
Records/watch 50
food   20
ticket 100
_____
        200
         100

KURT COBAIN JOURNALS

RIVERHEAD BOOKS
A MEMBER OF PENGUIN PUTNAM INC.
NEW YORK 2002

RIVERHEAD BOOKS
a member of
Penguin Putnam Inc.
375 Hudson Street
New York, NY 10014

Library of Congress Cataloging-in-Publication Data
Cobain, Kurt, 1967-1994.
Journals / Kurt Cobain.
p.   cm.
ISBN 1-57322-232-1
1. Cobain, Kurt, 1967-1994—Diaries.
2. Rock musicians—United States—Diaries.
ML420.C59 A3   2002   2002031690
782.42166'092—dc21
[B]

Printed in the United States of America

1 3 5 7 9 10 8 6 4 2

This book is printed on acid-free paper. ∞

ART DIRECTION & BOOK DESIGN BY CLAIRE VACCARO
DIGITAL PHOTOGRAPHY BY NICK VACCARO

Don't read my diary when I'm gone

OK, I'm going to work now, when you wake up this morning, please read my diary. Look through my things, and figure me out.

JOURNALS

Dale, count how many times i use the word "FUCK".

Hello, it is me saying

"everything is basically Raining, dull, and OK."
fuck we were this close ⟶
to coming down to see the melvins play on the
29th but as History Repeats itself, shelli being
the overbearing dominator of Chris decided to
not WANT to go at the last minute. and so
gas money being split only two ways between Tracy and I
would be too fucking expensive. are you coming to
Seattle someday to play? YOU MOTHERFUCKERS BETTER
STILL PLAY VILE VERMILLION VACANCY! or at least put it on the
Next LP. any label interest yet? Alchemy seems to be
in pretty sorry shape from what i hear. ever RAT SubCore
Dave Portnow? Dehumanizers? the reason i say this is
because they must be hard up, for they signed
DangerMouse! JESUSFUCKINGCHRISTALMighty

So within the last couple of months our demo
has been Pirated, Recorded, and discussed between all the
Seattle SCENE luminaries. and the Dude Johnathan
Poneman (Remember the guy who called me when you were
over the last day?) MR Big - money inheritance, Right
hand man of Bruce Pavitt. and also SUB POP Records
financial investor, got us a show at the vogue on a
Sub Pop sunday. Big Deal. but i guess hype and
Regularly being played on KCMU probably helped, the
amount of people who came to Judge us. Not be
at a BAR, Get drunk, watch some bands & have fun.
But just watch the show case event. 1 hr. We
felt there was a representative from every
Seattle band there just watching ⟶

OH OUR LAST AND FINAL NAME IS <u>**NIRVANA**</u>

ooH eeerie mystical Doom

We felt like they should have had score cards. And so after the set Bruce excitedly shakes our hands and says "wow Good job let's do A Record". ~~then~~ then flashes of cameras go off and this Girl from <u>BACKlash</u> says "Gee can we do an interview?" yeah sure why not. And then people say Good job you Guys are Great and Now we're expected to be total socialites. meeting people, introducing etc... **Fuck Im iN High SCHOOl AGAiN!** ~~I want to move back to Aberdeen.~~ NAH olympiA is just as boring and I can proudly say ive only been in the Smithfield About 5 times this year. And So because of this zoo-event we've At least gotten a contract for ₃₅₀ₙ₉ ~~A~~ single to be put out by end of August and an EP out in sept or oct. We're gonna try to talk them into an LP. Now Johnathan is ourmAnager, he gets us shows remotely in Oregon & Vancouver. He's paying for All recording & distribution costs & now ~~we~~ don't have to have outrageous phone Bills. Dave is working out OK. Sometime next year sub pop is gonna have A caravan of 2 or 3 seattle Bands go ontour. yeah we'll see. ■ Thru your past experiences Do you think it would be wise to demand receipts for recording, pressing costs?

Enough about records oh except this one night last month, Chris and I dropped acid And we were watching the late show (rip off of Johnny Carson) And PAul Revere And the RAiders were on there, they were so fucking stupid! Dancing around with moustaches, trying to Act comical and Goofy.

~~It~~ really pissed us off and I Asked Chris Do you ~~have~~ any paul Revere & the Raiders Albums?

2

YEAH punctuation, I was stoned alot when I was learning that stuff.

He said yeah, so I looked thru his Big collection and found the Revere Records and Busted them. and he got mad, then he laughed and I searched thru the rest of the Row and found Eagles, Carpenters, YES, Joni Mitchell and said with frustration, "What in the FUCK do you own these for? and so throughout the Rest of the night we busted about 250 shitty Chris Novoselic Records. not only did we clear more space in the living room, chris declared that he feels cleansed and revitalized.

I don't hang around with Ryan or the other Aberdonians but when im in town I'll get your Soundgarden Record for you. We still make movies, the last one we did was in Tacoma at NEVER NEVERLAND. it's a surrealistic fantasy story book place for kids, and we made shelli wear a mask of cher's head cut out of an album and dance around by big mushrooms and buttfuck the wolf bending over to blow down the three little pigs house. other stars included Rick Derringer and John lennons Penis. NO comment on Matts band MUDHONEY just to be on the safe side.
Speaking of safe sides my Girlfriend Tracy now has a Brand New "88" Toyota Turcell, a microwave, food processor, Blender, and an espresso machine, I don't have a job until next month thru TYSS youth service in a print shop part time, I AM A TOTALLY PAMPERED spoiled BUM NExt letter will be less boring about Record deals and more stupid drivel
GoodBye Dale write Soon.

The First song on the Demo is no longer played it is sickening and Dumb. Destroy it it is evil. in the likes of whitesnake and Bon Jovi.

The late 1980's.

This is A subliminal example of
a society that has sucked & fucked
itself into A Rehashing. VALue
of greed.

Subliminal in A sense that
there Are no P-Rock Collages
of michael J fox Reaming Bruce
SPRingsteen clinging to A missile.
instead the overall feeling that
you set
you Paid WAY too much for
you may say literally Nothing stimulating
yeah but other than the xerox the layout has A
Bull.   the Jokes on you   sense of professionalism
                    so
            kill yourself

No Amount of Effort can save you from

        oblivion.
        Power vomit magazine
        No Address
        No Editor
        No Ad Rates

                LOOK

Soundtrack to HR Puffnstuff
featuring MOMMA CASS
and JACK Wilde

Marlen Deitritch sings
Lilly marlene ←

e
hard th
s
C
Blin
Som
WAS
iri
An
And
the
Or
And
em
And
li
Blo
BAC
Doo
Jelly
m
fee
to

An
Yo

We Are willing to pay
for the majority of
pressing of 1000 copies of
our LP, And All of the
recording costs.   We
basically just want to
be on your label.
   Do you think you could
PLEASE! Send us A reply
of Fuck off, or Not interested
So we don't have to waste
more money sending more tapes?
thanks.   ~N pear
NIRVANA.

NIRVANA

_____

_____

_____

they weren't as gross as G.G. Allin but they
Held their own to say the least. The tension
grew because of a Delay with the P.A. which
Helped the Release of tension when the first
couple of notes of school were struck,
People instantly Rocked back and forth with
eyyes closed & beers clenched then
spilt. 5 Roadie friends had to lock arms
behind the P.A. Cabinets & Rockin in back & forth
in a wave
pushing the crowd in hopes that the band
wouldn't get hurt. But they did.
Kurdt the vocalist & Guitarist screamed
his last scream to the 2nd song then
Bam the crowd smacked the mike
into his mouth. Blood oozed from his
lip but they instantly started floyd the barber
After wiping kurts face, Chris the bass
player Accidentally hit kurt in the eye
with His Bass Headstock it wasn't too
deep At first until kurt Rammed his
Head into the wall next to him in
protest. it opened more. So kurdt
took his guitar & hit Chris straight in
the mouth causing a big cut lip. By now
they were pretty Bloody, Chris looking worse
And with only one wound. they were obviously
becoming dizzy and were in Pain. but
proceeded to play the set quite out of
tune

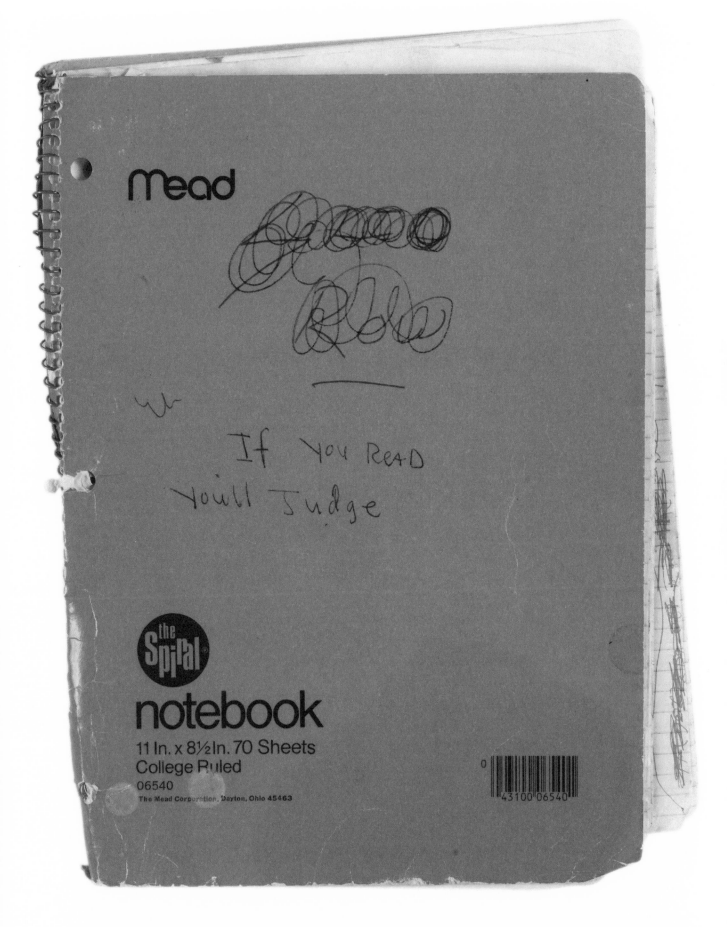

If You ReaD
You'll Judge

20 School Zones
25 Street of Cities & towns
50 County ROADS
55 HighwAy

PASS within **200** ft of Approaching cAr

Follow 20 ft for Every **10**. mph

TURN signal **100** ft before

Lane use Signals

☒ ☒
No   Yes
use   use

State   Federal   interstate

H WAY
intersection

Cross
ROAD
Right

Cross
ROAD
Left

Abrupt
end
of ROAD

Y intersection

DiviDeD
HighwAy

ends

ends

two
WAY

merge

clearance

PARK wheels DownHill TowArds Curb
12 inches legal PARK from Curb

Speed
- HighWAY 55
- Cities Towns 25
- School Zones 20
- County Roads 50

PASS within 200 ft of Approaching CAr

TurN Signal ON 100 ft before turning

Follow 20 ft for every 10 m.p.h.

FEDERAL (~~State~~)   State   interstate

CrossRoad to Left   Y intersection   Abrupt end   Cross Road to Right   4 way intersection

merge   two Lane Road   Divided Highway   clearance   end of Divided Highway

PArking

TurN wheels Towards curb when Parking

DownHill 12 in. AWAY from Curb

20 ft from intersection 30 signs Li

Dave,   5-29-88

    A band needs to practice, in our opinion,
at least 5 times a week if the band ever
expects to accomplish anything.
    We're tired of total uncertainty every time
we play a show, we think..."Are we going to
suck"? "Are we tight yet"? We have shows
and we don't practice! The two main reasons
are, Chris and his work and you and your
location. Chris can eventually alter his work
schedule and at least practice every week night.
    When we started with you, you claimed you could
make it up 4 times a week and would move up
here by July or August and it would be no
problem for you. We were very hesitant to
ever try this because of our experience with
driving back and forth to Aberdeen and we
knew it would eventually get on your nerves.
    We don't blame you at all for being tired
of driving, and we realize what a problem
and hassle it is to get someone else to
drive you up, but even if you could make
it up every day we don't start until 8:30 or
9:00, which is not enough time to even go
through the set. We know how long it takes
to build a house and you won't move up here
as soon as you have claimed, and in our
morals and values, fixing up a race car
isn't half as important as getting to practice
or recording or touring.

                              ⟶

We Also aren't convinced that you would get time off, or quit your job next winter to go on tour.   The overall aspect of this situation is nothing more than Selfish.   Getting a name on a record isn't shit. Anybody can do it, but theres a big difference between credentials & notoriety, and self respect through music.

Instead of lying to you by saying we're breaking up or letting this go any further we have to admit that we've got another drummer. His name is Chad, he's from Tacoma and he can make it to practice every night.   Most importantly, we can relate to him. lets face it, you are from a totally different culture.

Our hobbies and interests are different, and a band can't be a unit unless all the members are compatible.   We have really appreciated your loyalty and dedicated attempt at keeping this band alive.   You're a great drummer and we hope you pursue another band very soon.   We expect you to be totally pissed off and hate our guts and we don't blame you, because this is very sudden and we have not tried to warn you that this was happening. This is not your fault. It's ours. We should have known it wouldn't work, but your enthusiasm and clear headed thinking made us want to try it.   and we feel →

5-29-88

really shitty that we don't have the guts to tell you in person. But we don't know how mad you would All the luck to you and Laney get. and your drumming career. And if you wouldn't mind, we would like to suggest to other bands looking for drummers to check you out because your talent shouldn't go to waste.

please let us know when it is in your condevience for us to bring your drums & mic down. When you want to discuss this with us call. Sorry.
Kurt
chris

P.S. Lani - Thanks for driving Dave up all the time - I know what an awful drive it is. Shelli & I enjoyed spending time with you while they were practicing. Call us sometime & we can get together and do something.

— Tracy & Shelli

J.F.K: the lamest excuse ..er, retrogression

revolve
reverted   Reversion relapse   transpose

botanical   such High expectations, so much support,
growing   every ONe wants it more than me. Almost feel
               like doing it for them, Such high Aspirations,
               infinity doesnt exist. mathematics are based on 10.
               a number of special numeral variations eventually turn Synthesis
               of retrogression, Such being: reactive, cause and
               effect, communicational, scenario social interplay
               with situations within amongst people, music, sports,
               war, regional determination of botanical possibilities. Herbacious
               Hi, I dont have Dyslexia.   An infared light
               will simulate the sun in times of winter.
               A hypnotherapist will hold your hand and aid
               you into going back to bed. Downers & heroin
               make you itch.   If you talk to a friend, the
               friend will offer you a list of remedies that
               youve already tried.   The first seven years of
               my life were amazing, incredible, realistic and
               an absolute grateful joy.
                                                    ignore
               To be positive at all times is to erase all important
               and obsolete that is important, sacred or valuable.
               To be negative at all times is to be threatened
               by your rediculousness and instant discredibility.
rediculous   To translate opinions in an obvious search
               for proof of intelligence in the manor of abusive
manor   use   of obscure
               use with descriptive words is desperational
expression   will to sincere, yet retarded expression.

               I feel there is a universal sense amongst
               our generation that everything has been said
               and done. True.   but who cares
          it could still be fun to pretend.
               This is the first decade since the early 1940's that
               two generations listen to & share the same music.
                   (the old school and new school)

Dear mark,
Hello.   It sounds as if
everything is working out (sure) with Donna,
I cant wait to see & hear the
results!   Well i finally have
heard almost all of your albums,
except all of the beathappening/Trees EP
    I hope you dont mind but I
recorded them on the dreadful
    cassette tape. which is something
Im kind of against people doing, because
its not supporting the band . but
I swear! If I ever get a job Im
sure I'll buy all the records.
~~maybe even a tape~~
Well, on the back of the Clash's 1st LP
it says: home taping is killing the
music business [cassette]   oh! wow.
    This stuff on the tape (sent) is some 4tvk
mello pretty, sleep music, we've been
doing for the past couple of months.
    It's obvious that it has been inspired
from beathappening/ young Marble giants music.
    If you like some of it or if you have
something of your own in which you thought
I would be appropriate for the collaborating
then Im willing.

19

~~hopefully the~~ NIRVANA is planning on
Asking Calvin if he wants to put out A
(TC) Cassette of these songs & A couple
obscure heavy songs too.

   because ~~were~~ we feel like were
not Accomplishing Anything by
playing the Seattle club circuit
& It turns out that our single will
be out in Oct. (love buzz - big cheese.)
but there isnt much hope for An EP
within the near future, for SubPOP
is having financial problems And the
promise of An EP & LP within the year
was just A bullshit excuse for Johnathan
to keep us ~~there until that~~ from
scouting other labels. & so here it is
8 months later & we finally put out
A damn single. Weve sent the demo
to A few labels. but no Response.

   So if you have Any numbers
or Addresses or if you meet someone
& give them A demo It would be
greatly Appreciated. we have About
30 bulk recording tapes & Any postage
& handling will be gladly paid.
we just feel like were becoming Stagnant
in olympia with no record.

Just before I fall asleep and
when I'm really bored I... laydown and
think for awhile until I ~~subconciously go~~ fall
into a ~~type~~ semi hypnotic state of sub-
-conciousness, some call it daydreaming, some
call it just fucking spacing out. but i feel like
I'm not here and it doesn't matter because I'm
sick of putting myself in boring situations and
pre~~mgmentory~~ conversations, just every day
basic sit com happenings, some call it thinking
but when im ~~think I forget to think~~ in this
particular state of mind i forget to think and it
becomes strictly observatory. I notice things
very sensitively like if i focus really hard
I can see small transparent blotches of
~~dirt~~ debris on the outer shell of my eyes.
(or the conjunctiva). and can only follow it
as my eye moves downward, its like, watching
film footage of amoeba or jelly like
plankton under a microscope. and when
I close my eyes and look up to the sun
the bright orange redness radiates an
intense picture of blood cells or what I
think are blood cells. and they are moving
very rapidly and again I can only focus for
so long before my eyes strain and I have
to look away from the sun int a pillow, can
and rub my eyes hard then I see some call
them stars
Tiny spheres of sparkling light which only
stay for a second then as my eyes focus
→

Again ~~Amidst~~ Amongst the Water or Tears from rubbing I open then look up to the sky AWAY from THE SUN And ~~forget~~ About stupid fucking little squiggly things moving on the outer laver of my eyes or the ~~B~~ close up Blood cells in my eye lids And I stare At the ~~cloud~~ SKY with perrifial vision And not trying but just ~~to~~ happening to make out All kinds of faces objects statues in the clouds And I can do the same with the wood grain of the panelling on my walls. ~~And so what.~~

Once I saw Jesus on A Tortilla shell.

UNCERTAINTY like opening your eyes wide in the dark then closing them hard then open and blinded by the sparkling silver dots created from pressure on the corneas, squint, Roll, focus, then your Blind again but at least you saw light somehow.. maybe ~~it was tored~~ the light was stored in the sockets or held in the iris or clung to the tips of all the nerves and veins. Then your eyes close again and an artificial light appears before the eyelids, probably just a light bulb or a Blowtorch! jesus its hot! my lashes and brows are curling up and melting emiting the worst smell of burnt hair and thru the Red Transparency of the light in my eyelids I can see a close up view of Blood cells move as I move my eyes back and forth like footage of a documentary of amoeba and plankton jelly like ~~see~~ thru life forms moving man they must be small I cant feel them my eyes must be able to see things MORE clearly than ~~I had~~ expected it's like a microscope but it doesn't matter anymore cause they set me on fire now yep I'm sure of it I'm on fire God damn it.

In a last attempt to make it clear ~~how~~
that this girl did not have downs syndrome
or a mongoloid, ~~there~~ is proof that ~~Lakeside~~ High school
does not ~~have~~ or ever has had the facilities to
~~teach~~ those cronic retards. ~~And~~ in fact Darrin,
Ace, and Trevor were also in one of her classes
& she also had regular classes for normal people.
    A lot of naive asshole kids just called her
retarded because she never talked. ~~Which ~~
~~you will find out later in the story how our~~
~~association with her was so badly labeled~~
~~& mistaken~~
        The object of the guys who had been
going there for the past month was to steal
booze from the down stairs basement den..
while ~~one~~ others distracted her by opening
~~Her room~~ cupboard doors & pretending to eat all the
food, one would go down & take a 5th
& then exit out the downstairs.
        It was basically a gift to Trevor the
pot overlord who enjoyed pot not quite as much
as booze, and to his helpers & I a
reward of getting high in the woods near
the school was always promised if we
stold booze for him.   Only being stoned
within that week for the first few times was
what I claimed as "something I will do
for the rest of my life!"   And I would practically
do anything to ensure my supply of the fantastic
weed ~~pot~~.   So we did this routine every other day
        & got away with it for ~~quite a long~~
about a month   →

And during that month I happened to be the
Epitomy of my mental abuse from my mother.
~~The ~~ ~~before.~~   It turned out that pot didn't
help me escape my troubles too well any more
And I was actually enjoying doing rebellious
things like stealing this booze & busting
store windows getting in fist fights etc....
& nothing even mattered.   I decided withing
the next month I'll not sit on my roof and
think about jumping but ill actually kill myself
And I wasn't going out of this world without
actually knowing what it is like to get laid.
      So one day after school I went to
her house alone, and invited myself in
and she offered me some twinkies and I sat
on her lap and said "let's fuck" and I
touched her tits and she went into her bedroom
and got undressed in front of me with the
door open and I watched & realized that
it was actually happening so I tried to
fuck her but didn't know how and asked her
if she had ever done this before and she said
a lot of times mainly with her cousin.
      I got grossed out very heavily with how
her vagina smelled & her sweat reaked so
I left.   My concience grew to where I
couldn't go to school for a week and when i
went back I got in-house suspetion in the
office for skipping and that day the girls
father came in screaming & accusing someone
of taking advantage of his daughter

& they went in the ~~off~~ principals office And yelled At eAchother & they came out with a yearbook & were going to have her pick me out. but she couldn't because I ~~was~~ didn't show up for pictures that year. & so during lunch the rumors stArted And by the next day she told my nAme And everyone WAS WAiting for me to yell & cuss & spit At me calling me the retard fucker'.

Because A lotof people liked me the sides were even but I couldn't handle the ridicule so on A SAturdAy night I got high & drunk & walked down to the train tracks & lAyed down & wAited for the 11:00 train & I put 2 big pieces of cement on my chest & legs & the train came closer & closer.

And it went on the next trAck beside me instead of over me. So I rode the bus to ~~Jenkins Lane~~ LAkeside School from ~~Jenkins Lane~~ every day pretending to go to school & doing Acid instead walking in the woods, So my mom would think I WAS going to school & the cops stopped me one night At A football gAme & I went down to the stAtion & they tApe recorded my confession of what I did And sAid that ~~her~~ family cAn't do Anythin, ~~because~~ she WAS 18 And not mentally retArded. But tension from school mAde me have to Attent ~~Jenkins 1k~~ school And the train scared me enough to try to rehabilitAte myself & my GuitAr ~~seemed to~~ playing seemed to be improving so I became less manically depressed but still never HAd Any friends because I hAted everyone for they were so phony.

NIRVANA is from Olympia WA, 60 miles from Seattle. NIRVANAS Guitar/vocalist (Kurt Kobain) And Bass-(Chris Novoselic) lived in Aberdeen 190 miles from Seattle.

Aberdeens population Consists of Highly bigoted Redneck. snoose chewing - deer shooting, faggot killing - logger types who "Ain't to ~~fond~~ partial to weirdo NEW WAVers!" (Chad) drums is from An island of Rich Kid-L.S.D Abusers.

NIRVANA is A trio who play Heavy Rock with Punk overtones.

They usually dont have jobs.

So they can tour anytime.

NIRVANA HAS never jammed on Gloria, or Louie Louie. NOR have they ever had to Re write these songs & call them their own.

NIRVANA is looking to put their music to Vinyl or Accepting A loan of About $2,000.oo.

Kurdt

<u>Lance Link</u>
After Beat happening

Crybaby & Richard Simmons

Hot Dog eating contest

✳ Penis Balloon insertion
for erection

✳ light bulb swallower
Rem
H Rollins
L Lunch
TARDS
Bill murray lounge
Stairway to Heaven

✳ DAVEY & GOLIATH
Bros QUAY
Spoons magnets BABY

✳ monster tard movie

Jesse Hello,

Believe me, I have purposely been
delaying writing you for a while so
when our single finally comes out I
could send it to you as well as a letter.
But God time flies. and Sub Pop
is broke and full of shit. And I didn't
realize how long its been since I
Received your letter. So I'm sorry!

Hey Cheer up dude, your letter
sounded like you're kinda bored.

I can't wait until you come down
for Christmas, it will be the most
exciting ~~$~~ event this year. We got
our test pressings back for the single. I've
been waiting for so long that I'm not
even ~~worried about~~ looking forward to it coming out. We've
Refused to do anything else with Sub Pop
even though they really want us to put out an
EP. We've decided to put out our own
LP. We found a record pressing plant that
will press 1000 records for $1,600.00. So At
$8.00. a piece we only have to sell about
250 records to get our money back, And
the rest is pure profit, then All we
have to do is find a distributor.
We played with the Butthole surfers. And
then D.O.A in seattle. The melvins are coming
back to play a couple shows with us.

Chris and shelli broke up. God am I
relieved! she is still living in Tacoma

And Chris is temporarily staying in Aberdeen for free at his moms. I'm very content with the relationship Chris, chad and I have, we get along great and have a lot of dedicated fun. We are becoming very well received in Seattle & other places in Wash. Promoters call us up to see if we want to play, instead of us having to hound people for shows. Its now just a matter of time for labels to hunt us down, now that we've promoted ourselves pretty good by doing small remote tours. OK. enough about the band.

I've got a janitor job, working with this older guy cleaning 4 restaurants. Pays cash under the table part time.

Tracy and I get along just fine, as usual. lately I've found myself becoming lazy. I hardly write any stories and I don't work on songs quite as intently as in the past. You know why? ? ?

Television Television is the most evil thing on our planet.

Go right now to your TV and toss it out the window, or sell it and buy a better stereo. I have the flu right now so I don't feel like conjuring up witty literature. my eyes burn & when I fart, hot bubble acid ooze squirts from my

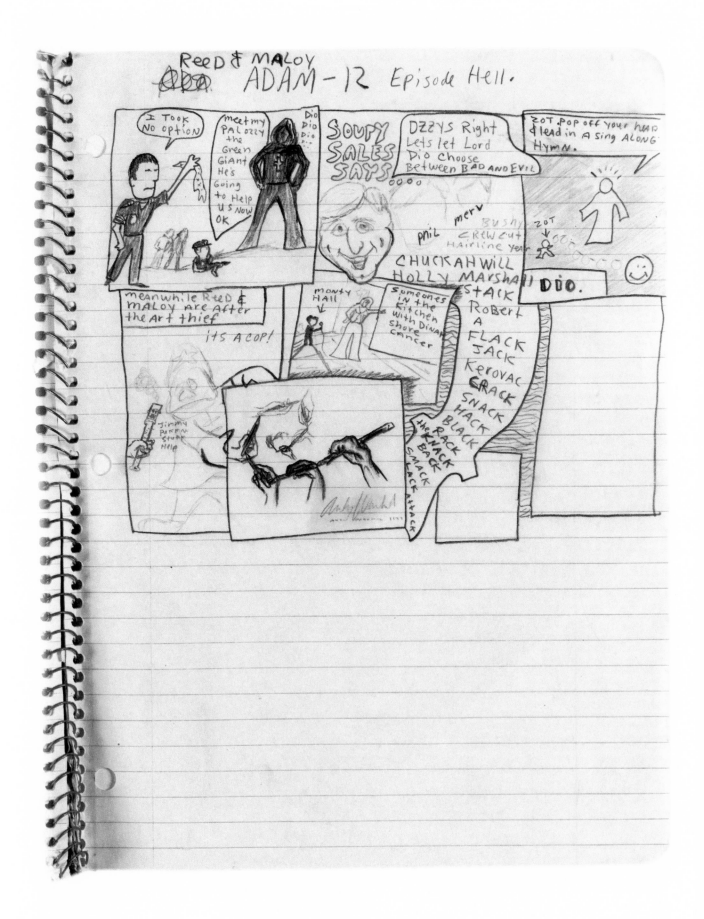

Greetings,

NIRVANA is a three piece spawned from the bowels of a Redneck ~~loser town called~~ Aberdeen WA. and ~~the~~ a hippie commune ~~from~~ on Bainbridge ~~Island~~ Island. Only together for 7 months Kurdt-Guitar vocals - Chris bass & Chad-Drums have acquired a single on Sub Pop Records (A song in Sub Pop 200 comp,) a Demo, success & fame & a following of millions. Selling their bottled sweat & locks of hair have proven to be the largest money maker so far, but in futurei dolls, peechees, lunch boxes & bed sheets are in the works. AN LP is due ~~this~~ April from the wonderful ~~head~~ offices of Sub Pop world headquarters. talent Agents bruce Pavitt (alias Henry Mancini) and Johnathan Poneman (alias fred flintstone) have "treated the boys good" and the boys hope to work on more projects in the future. with them

NIRVANA sounds like black sabbath - playing the KNACK, Black Flag, Led Zeppelin, & the stooges, with a pinch of Bay City Rollers. their musical influences are: H.R. Puffnstuff, ~~speed~~ Marine Boy, Divorces, Drugs, Sound effects Records, the Beatles, Young Marble Giants, Slayer, leadbelly, IGGY,

NIRVANA sees the underground music SEEN as becoming, stagnant and more Accessible towards commercial Major Label interests. Does NIRVANA want to change this? No way! We want to cash in & suck butt up to the big wigs in hopes that we too can get high & fuck wax figure-hot babes, who will be required to have a certified Aids test 2 weeks prior to the day of handing out back stage passes. Soon we will need chick spray Repellant. Soon we will be coming to your town & Asking if we can stay at your house & use your stove. Soon we will do encores of Gloria & louie louie at benefit concerts with all our celebrity friends

We Realize that there ~~was~~ once a 60's band called NIRVANA but dont get us ~~mixed~~ confused with them because they totally suck big fucking Dick.

Good Bye.

N Pear olympia wy 98500

"SAFER THAN HEAVEN"

NIRVANA

GREETINGS,

NIRVANA is a three piece spawned from the bowels of a redneck - logger town called Aberdeen WA, and a hippie commune on Bainbridge island.

Although only together for seven months KurDt-guit-voc, Chris-bass and Chad-drums have acquired a single on Sub Pop records, one cut on the Sub Pop 200 compilation, a demo, an LP in April, success, fame and a following of millions.

Selling their bottled sweat and locks of hair have proven to be their biggest money makers so far, but in the future: dolls, pee chees, lunch boxes and bed sheets are in the works.

From the wonderful offices of Sub Pop world headquarters our talent agents Bruce Pavitt and Johnathan Poneman have treated the boys good.

NIRVANA hope to work on more projects with them in the future.

NIRVANA sounds like: Black Sabbath playing the Knack, Black Flag, Led ZEP, the Stooges and a pinch of Bay city Rollers.

Their personal musical influences include: H.R Puffnstuff, Marine boy, divorces, drugs, sound effect records, the Beatles, Young Marble Giants, Slayer, Leadbelly and Iggy.

NIRVANA sees the underground music SEEN as becoming stagnant and more accessible towards commercialized major label interests.

Does NIRVANA feel a moral duty to change this cancerous evil?

No way! We want to cash in and suck butt of the big wigs in hopes that we too can GET HIGH and FUCK. GET HIGH and FUCK. GET HIGH and FUCK.

Soon we will need chick repellant spray. Soon we will be coming to your town asking if we can stay over at your house and use your stove.

Soon we will do encores of Gloria and Louie Louie at benefit concerts with all our celebrity friends. NIRVANA c/o SUB POP 1932 1st AVE..#1103. Seattle WA 98101 or

Thank you for your time.

FUCK NOW, SUFFER LATER

GREETINGS,

NIRVANA is a heavy-pop/punk/dirge-combo spawned from the bowels of Seattle Washington.

Although only together for seven months KURDT Guitar/voc, CHRIS-bass, CHAD- drums and JASON-guitar have acquired a single, an LP entitled "Bleach", one cut on the SUB POP 200 compilation, sucess, fame and a following of millions.

Selling their bottled sweat and lochs of hair have proven to be their biggest money makers so far, and in the future: dolls, pee-chees, lunch boxes and bed sheets are in store.

From the towering offices of SUB POP world headquarters our talent agents Johnathan Poneman and Bruce Pavitt have treated the boys swell.

NIRVANA hope to produce more projects with them in the future.

NIRVANA sounds like mid-tempo Black Sabbath playing the Knack, Black Flag, the Stooges with a pinch of Bay City Rollers.

Their personal musical influences include: H.R. Puffnstuff, Speed Racer,DIVORCES, drugs, sound effects records, the beatles, rednecks, asorted hard rock, old punk rock, Leadbelly, Slayer and of course the Stooges.

NIRVANA sees the underground SeeN as becoming stagnant and more accessible towards commercialized major label interests.

Does NIRVANA feel a moral duty to change this cancerous evil?

NO way! We want to CASH IN and SucK UP to the big wigs in hopes that we too can GET HIGH AND FUCK GET HIGH AND FUCK.GET HIGH AND FUCK.

SOON we will need groupie repellant spray. SOON we will be coming to your town asking if we can stay over at your house and use the stove. SOON we will do encores of GLORIA and LOUIE LOUIE at benefit concerts with all our celebrity friends.

NIRVANA c/o SUB POP 1932 1st ave. # 1103. Seattle Wa 98101 or
Thank you for your time.

S·U·B P·O·P

MARK,
    WHOA! Polly Perreguin is
my favorite song as of this decade.
I've been soaking up the sounds of
the Screaming Trees for a few
months and ~~●~~ I think it's way
better than most, although in the
pop genre I like pixies &
 Smithereens a bit better. But
Polly Perreguin, ~~Jeezus~~ GOD!
What a complete masterpiece.
 Hey hows tour? oh. Donna seems
to fit in just fine. I predict
the mighty Major label in the future
for you people. Heres some well,
fuck, I must admit screaming Trees
influenced pop weve been experimenting
with.   we played with the Butthole Surfers,
they wouldnt move their drums. Jeesus!
Got paid 75.00 whole dollars.
    Sub Pop is always broke. So were
openly looking for any other offer. They
mean well but we don't feel its fair
for mudhoney to be favored & catered
to a higher level than the other bands.
Oh well. ~~●●●●●●●●●●●●●●●●●●~~ we want
to tour in March, if you have any #'s
or suggestions, we would appreciate
any Help.

NIRVANA

Kenichewa

Dear

NIRVANA IS A three piece from
the Outskirts of Seattle WA.

Kurdt-Guitar/voice and Chris-bass have
struggled with too many un dedicated drummers
for the past 3 years, performing under
such names as: Bliss, throat Oyster, Pen Cap Ch.
Ted ed Fred ETC.. for the last 9
months we have had the pleasure to
take Chad-drums under our wings and
develop what we are now and always
will be **NIRVANA**.

3 regularly broadcasted carts on K.C.M.U
(Seattle College Radio also KAOS olympia)
Played with: Leaving Trains, Whipping Boy,
Hell's Kitchen, Treacherous JayWalkers &
Countless local acts.

Looking for: EP or LP   We have about
15 songs Recorded on 8 Tracks at
Reciprocal studios in Seattle.

Willing to compromise on material (some
of this shit is pretty old)   Tour Any-
-time forever hopefully the music will speak for itself
Please Reply THANK YOU   Area code
                               (206)
           N. Pear olympia VA. 98506

37

Things the band needs to do

① Send some fucking demo tapes
get chad to fucking fork over
some money.

② PRESS Kit
  1) get ahold of charles and Alice
  to get some pictures
  2) have Tam write out a story line
  3) then copy them off. ~~Simple~~ !

③ Find a practice place

④ Call NANN WARSAW in Chicago. ask if
she has any connections with Touch-n-go
Also ask for ~~a list~~ her to send a list of
prominent MAgazines & Record stores that
We could make contacts With.

⑤

AT <u>EVERY</u> stop yo<u>u mus</u>t check:
1 OIL   7. PACK Bearings
2 WAter   8. check lights
3 Air pressur 9. lug nuts
4 transmission 10. WASH VAN
5 Battery WAter 11. Radiator Hose
6 Brake fluid 12. Windows
   *LOCK ALL DOORS

<u>NO</u> Guests, groupies, Band members etc.

<u>NO</u> use of Any Gas Corporation services
   Besides EXXON.   NO exceptions

Every 400 miles there will be An
inspection check of VAN cleAnliness
And equipment Count.
Find a safe place to pull over And
take every piece of musical
equipment out: refer to <u>musical</u>
~~equip~~electronic pamphlet in glove compartment.

part time Janitorial position

in the olympian newspaper

7 months At lemons Janitorial
pyear At polynesian condominium resort
in Ocean Shores
2 summers work At Aberdeen YMCA
& Weathermax High school

& 9 months At lamplighter restaurant
in Grayland WA.

13   4   6 — 10
                      5

        4.00/hr   Nov—

2½ yrs experience

Lemons Janitorial   sept 87 - feb 88
Basic Route cleaning buildings $4.50/hr

Polynesian Condominium hotel Resort   ocean shores $5.00/hr
Sept - 86 - June 87   C/o Betty Kaales (housekeeping)
~~Custoda~~ maintenance ~~job~~   basic odd jobs, windows
Carpet cleaning,   moved to olympia

Aberdeen Y.M.C.A   C/o Alfie Bensinger $3.35/hr
~~April~~ May 86 - ~~August~~ sept. 86
lifeguard, preschool swimming instructor, day care
baseball coach, maintenance.   summer temporary employment

Lamplighter Restaurant   grayland WA $4.25/hr
sept 85 - March 86   C/o   Bud ~~Turley~~ & Audrey Turley
dishwasher, prep, clean up, busperson

(Coast building
  10029 So TACOMA WAY
  off exit   behind
  127   TACOMA Cody's Restaurant)

42

Pine ~~Fresh~~ Tree

Janitorial Service

Commercial

Basic commercial maintenance

PINE TREE

Janitorial Service

Kurt

Chris

friendly, prompt,
& clean.

Commercial maintenance

bathrooms - ~~sink~~ toilet - mop - mirrors - Paper towel/
TP-supply. Office - Dust - vacuum - sweep - ashtrays -
- Garbage - windows -
We purposely limit our number of commercial offices
in order to ~~take time. And personally clean~~
personally clean while taking our time. We
guarantee $50.00 lower rates, than your present
janitorial service.
You see, other ~~complet~~ services usually have
too many buildings assigned to the individuals Route:
so in turn they end up Running thru buildings trying
for time. but AT Pine Tree —

43

my lyrics are a big pile of contradictions.
they're split down the middle between
very sincere opinions and feelings that I have
and sarcastic and hopefully — humorous
rebuttles towards cliché — bohemian ideals
that have been exhausted for years.

I mean it seems like there are only two
options for personalities for songwriters either
they're sAd, tragic visionaries like morrisey
or michael Stipe or Robert Smith. or there's
the goofy, Nutty white boy, Hey, lets party
and forget everything people like vAn HAlen
or All that other heavy maetal crap

I mean I like to be pAssionate and
Sincere, but I also like to have
fun and act like a dork.
 Geeks unite.

DOWNER

1
PORTRAY SINCERITY ACT OUT of LOYALTY
Defend your free Country-wish AWAY PAIN
HAND OUT lobotomys to SAVE little familys
SurreAlistic fantAsy BlAnd Boring   plAin

2
Holy Now IN Restitution - living out our DAte-
with FUSION - IN our whole fleece shun in
BAstard- dont feel guilty mAster writing

3
Somebody sAys thAt their not much like I AM
I know I CAN - mAke enough up the words AS
you Go Along I siNG then some.

4
Sickening pesimist hypocrite mAster
ConserUAtive Communist Apocalyptic BAstard.
ThAnk you DeAr GoD for putting me on this EArth
I feel very priviledged iN debt for my thirst

2   and   3

floyd the Barber

Bell oN Door ClaNks- Come oN IN

floyd observes my HAiry ChiN

Sit dowN ChAir dont Be AfrAid

STeAmed HoT Towel oN my fACe

    I   WAS   ShAved (3x^s)

BarNey Ties me to the chAir

I caNt see Im ReAlly scAred

floyd BreAthes hard I hear A zip

Pee Pee pressed AGAiNst my lips

    I   WAS   ShAmed (3x^s)

I sense others iN the Room

Opey AuNt Bee I PResume

they TAke TurNs iN CuT me uP

I died smothered iN ANdys Butt

    I   WAS   ShAved (3x^s)

PAPER CUTS

When.. my feeding TiME
She push food thru the Door
I crawl towards the CRACKS of Light
Sometimes I cant find my WAY

~~conta~~

newspapers spread Around
SOAKING All that they Can
A Cleaning is due AGAIN
~~INCREASING CLOUDS OF RAIN~~

A Good HOSING DOWN

The LADy whom I feel A maternal Love for
Cannot look me in the eyes. But I see
hers And they Are Blue And they Cock And
Twitch And masturbate

~~why - Because ou~~ I SAID So - I SAID So - I SAID So

A Reason   A Reason   A Reason   ~~Try~~ Try AGAIN

BLACK windows Are PAINT
I Scratch with my NAILS
I See others just like me
why do they NOT Try escape?

They bring out the older ones
They point At my WAY
The older ones Come with lights
And TAKe my family AWAY

CoNT. →

PAper Cuts
Continued

And very later I have learned to Accept some friends of Ridicule - my whole existence was for your Amusement And that is why Im Here with you

To TAKe You - with me TO - your eyes are Blue ~~Believe~~ Relief to   NIRVANA

NIRVANA   NIRVANA   NIRVANA

NIRVANA   NIRVAWA   NIRVANAAAH

HAIRSPRAY QUEEN

① I WAS your mind • You were my my ene me
You were mine • I WAS WAS your ene me
You would mind • I WAS your your ene me
You were mine • I WAS WAS your enA

EARS   RAN G   2x's
          ①

② AT Night • the wishfull Goddess • AT Night
Shell wish the HARdest • AT Night the Disco
Goddess • AT Night the witch go gosh

①
②
(Voice ① DRoned)

AT Night • the wishful Goddess • AT Night
Shell wish the HARdest • AT Night •
the Disco Goddess • AT Night •
the itch so modest • AT Night •
the Crisco loch Ness • AT Right •
the mouthfull omelette • AT Sight
the fishfull goBlets • AT Night the witch go
          GAAAAAAAAAAWD

49

Mexican Seafood

AH the itchy flakes it is A flaming
All the Gels and cremes it is pertaining
to A fungus mold cured by injection
Hope it's only AH A Yeast infection

② OH well it burns when I — it hurts when
I pee — OH well it hurts when I — it hurts
when I see.

Now I vomit cum and diahrrea
on the tile floor like oatmeal pizza
fill my toilet bowl full of A cloudy puss
I feel the Blood becoming chowder rust

②

Roll into my Bed which does consist of
lice Bugs and fleas and yellow mucus
stained dirt VASaline Toe Jam & Booger
stomach Acid worms that Dance in
sugared sludge

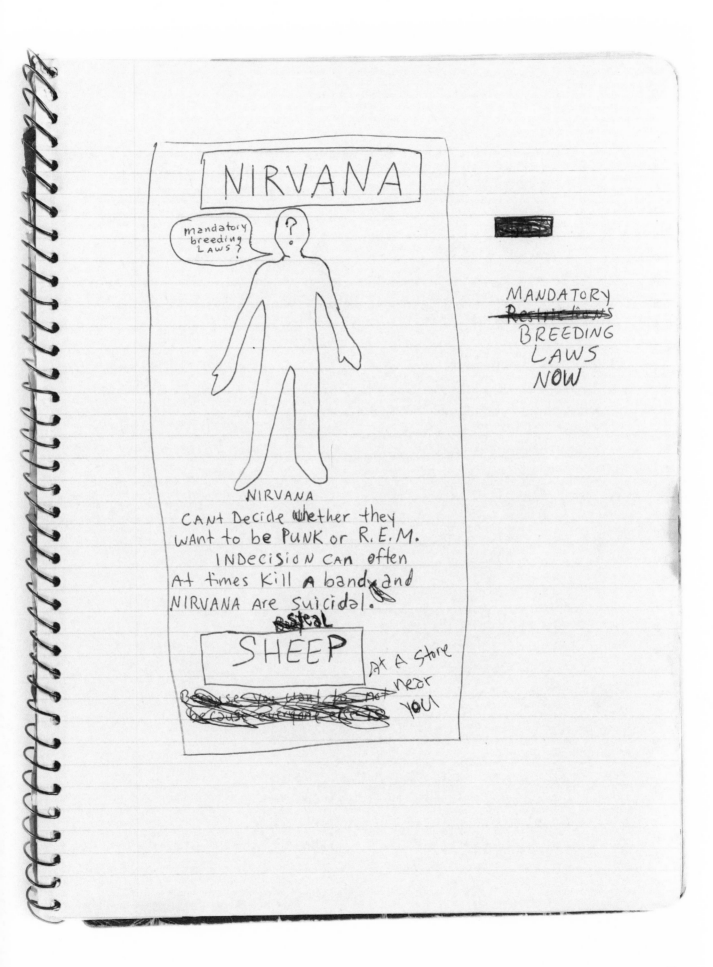

MANDATORY
~~Restrictions~~
BREEDING
LAWS
NOW

NIRVANA

The KKK Are the
only NIGGErS.

MAy women rule
the world.

Abort christ.

AssAsinate the
Greater And Lesser
of two evils.

steal
SHEEP

At A store near
You.

NIRVANA

Flowers
perfume
CAndy
puppies
Love
Generational
Solidarity
And
Killing Your
parents

SHEEP

NIRVANA

~~10 GrAmmy~~
3 time GrAnny award winners,
NO. 1 on billbored top 100
for 36 consecutive weaks
in A row.   2 times on
the cover of Bowling stoned,
HAiled as the most original,
thought provoking and important band
of our decade by Thyme & Newsweak

Pen Cap Chew

OH lesser God OH loAthe me
OH lesser God OH Your lonely
OH lesser God OH Bore me
OH lesser God OH   OH

You get You get You get You get to me
Holy is the time it's such an eAsy WAy to go

You get You get You Get - You get to Be
Hide the struggle in the Skin under A
    finger nAil

OH lesser god OH loAthe me OH lesser god OH lonely
OH lesser god OH loAthe me OH lesser Dog OH lonely

WAste Your time By sAving Worthless Gullables
Kill A Pollitiian And then weAr his Clothes
this decade is the Age of Re-HAshing
Protest And then go to JAil for Tresspassing
        Go   Home (4x's)

CAn You see the ReAson for My EntroPe
Is there something wrong Without society
HAs Your Concience got to You for Building
Trends - is thAt Why unoticing You
    EAt Your Pens?

        Go Home   (8x's)

53

Aeroszeppelin

Whats a season in a right
If you can't have anything
Whats the reason in a rhyme
If a plan means anything
Whats the meaning in a crime
It's a fan if anything
Wheres a leaning in a line
It's a BRAND   It's a BRAND ██████████

How a culture comes again
It was all here yesterday
And you swear it's not a trend
Doesn't matter anyways
They're only here to talk to friends
Nothing new is every day
You could shit upon the stage   they'll be fans
if you brand if you brand if you brand

All the kids will eat it up -
if it's packaged properly
Steal a sound and imitate
Keep a format equally
not an ode
just the facts
Where our world is nowadays
An idea is what we lack
it doesn't matter anyways

MELVINS

I remember ~~painfully~~ painfully   you
                                                        saucy upstart

Gyuto monks

if you need an explenation on what montsano
is like, refer to any NIRVANA article of the past
3 years on the subject of Aberdeen, the two
coastal logging slumps are similar in the lack of
cultural   and ~~music~~ good musical availability

~~I'm tired of people saying~~ the melvins don't get the recognition they deserve

melvins when they finally get the recognition they deserve

they can look forward to ~~~~~~ un punk rock adoration
~~adoration~~ (late) from fans waiting outside the venue waiting for autographs

The true adoration that matters is one they have already
but the small amount of fanatics who are into them already

~~I remember~~ when the melvins played Jimi Hendrix & Cream songs
~~Hell they weren't the melvins~~ ~~then~~

them
festival   ~~I remember:~~ when the melvins played lightning speed melodic,
punk rock hardcore ~~~~ with typewriter drumming.
                 then they
~~then they played~~ started slowing down with a mix of stutas
Black flag   ~~of~~ melodic sabbath like   abrasion
damage II
               excitedly
~~then~~ Buzz came over with Black flag My War
~~he told this is the best~~ claiming it was ~~the best~~ as important
as

. their habit was financed by their earnings of pizza & bus boy Jobs

During the summer month of the U.S. festival in 84

I remember in the summer of 82 or 83 there was this extravaganza of a rock-like woodstock Concert held in some far away exotic land featuring all the contemporary Hard rock acts like AC DC or Van Halen. To the stoner world it was a big deal but for me it was Something a joke I didn't pay much attention to it but I remember my friends staring up to the sky during the weeks prior to this Gathering with a tear of empty unattainable dreams that this festival is never to be a part of their hanging out of the smoker shed reality. in other words there wasn't a chance in hell that they'll save up enough pot money to make the long trek to the fatherland promise land of the U.S festival

I remember hanging out at a montesano Washingtons thriftway when this short haired employee employee boxboy who kinda looked like the Guy in Air Supply handed me a flyer that reads: the Them festival. tomorrow night in the parking lot behind Thriftway

free **live** Rock music

Montesano WAshington a place not accustomed to having live rock acts in their little village A population Af a few thousand loggers and their subservient wives

~~I~~ showed up with stoner friends in a van
we pulled into the parking lot behind the
Thriftway Another zombies ~~congregated~~ Slouch bobbed with combs in their BACK pockets
~~sit~~ There stood the Air supply box boy ~~sit~~
a ~~picture~~ holding a les paul with A picture
from A magazine of Kool cigarettes lamenated on it a mechanic
redheaded biker boy and ~~that~~ the "talkin guy", the first
to ever wear skin tight levis, a bold and brave
change from sticky finger or Sanfrancisco riding Gear.
    They played faster than I had ever imagined
music could be played and with more energy than
my iron Maiden records could provide, this
was ~~what~~ I ~~was~~ looking. for, AH punk ROCK
    The other stoners were Bored and ~~kept~~
~~asking them~~ kept shouting, play some
Def Leppard. God I hated those fucks more
than ever I came to the promise land
of A Grocery store I, found my special purpose the next day I
spiked ~~my~~ the upper part of my head, but
I couldn't quite part with my stoner roots and the long hair in
the back, thus developing the first Bi level
haircut in montesano history, I walked around
for a week looking like rod stewart. I started
following the melvins around. I was the
Quiet tag along. one day they even let
me try out for the band but I was

way too nervous and during the next few
years as I watched buzz transform from
typewriter drumming, speed core to
the constepation blues stemmed from the
influence of Black flag, my war,
     ST Vitus and a short lived stint with
various metal Blade recording artists. something
new was H ~~much transforming~~ Buzz do this
     thru a few years of ~~study~~ internally personal
developments of strict morals niche like and opinions
sincere devotion to the celebration of ~~energy~~ and the appreciation
of spirituality ~~and sincere~~ Buzz stays true
to his school, giving off an air of if you even
think of me compromising I'll Kill you attitude   Narcoleptic
rolling his ~~eyes~~ eyes to the back of the head   (epileptic)
                                                       little boy
pissing sweat in Aritually Autistic (sway   rocking back n forth disease?
downstroking muffled lowest notes possible chunk
chopping block, Cuttural bowel drones.
     harmonic satanic and uh heavy. low
     Deep Cool man cool Goddamn the pusher man.
     A lot of Mohawks said I used to like the meluns
until they became Black Sabbath Jeez ~~that~~ A typically
clever observation

So I sat in the corner at hundreds of
melvins practices

The MeLVINS Are Alive

WORDS suck. I mean, every thing has been said. I cant remember the last real interesting conversation ive had in a long time. WORDS arent as important as the energy derived from music, especially live. I dont think ive ever gotten any good descriptions from lyric sheets, except WHITE ZOMBIE whos lyrics remind me that theres only so many words in the English language, and most good imagery has been used, as well as good band names, LP titles and not to mention the bloody music itself. GEE, I dont want to sound so negative but were dealing with the MELVINS. IN one live MELVINS performance you wont be able to understand very many words, as is with any band) but you will FEEL the negative ENERGY. Music is ENERGY. A mood, atmosphere. FEELING. The MELVINS have and always will be the king pins of EMOTION. Im not talking about fucking stupid human compassion, this is one of the only real istic reminders that every day we live amongst VIOLENCE. There is a time and place for this music. So if you want to shake your groove thang to simple primal rock, then go see a fucking bar band! The MELVINS aint for you. And they probably dont want ya.

Like I said im not too hip on lyrics, so I didnt ask them about lyrics. Aparently their lyrics are almost equally important as the music. In their case I have to agree, even though I can hardly decipher any of the words, I can sense they display as much emotion as the music and therefore I hypocritically plead to you "BUZZ", On the next record have a lyric sheet, and if you need, have an explanation for every line. Im shure a lot of kids would dig it. man.

Speaking of BUZZ, he looks better in an afro than that guy in the movie CAR WASH. Im thinking he should take advantage of this blessing and be the first to go beyond the hip hops shaved symbols and architectured genious of scalp artistry and SCULPt a wacky far out cactus or Bull Winkle antlers.

He writes the songs, riffs first, lyrics second and goddamn is they good! Hes an all around nice guy.

DALE lost weight, bleached and chopped his hair. He plays even harder and an all around NICE GUY.

LORI kicks John Entwistles butt, and is all around nice guy.

They enjoy the GYUTO MONKS , Tibetan Tantric choir. One of the only forms of religious communication in which I have been emotionally affected by along with the MELVINS and uh maybe the STOOGES or SWANS raping a slave EP'. The only good thing MICKEY HART ever did was to bring this sacred group of monks on a tour in which ive heard from many, seemed like an impersonal circus or freak show. Oh well they needed money to build a new monestary. They probably didnt notice the yochie dead heads hanging out in the audience. yuk!

The special technique in the monks vocalization is a long study of producing three notes or a full chord in the form of long droning chants. It makes for a soothing eerie feeling.

This is an interview that was written several months
after matt left the Band in ~~se~~ oct.

are you satisfied with the new line up of the melvins.
and where you live?

are you ~~feel~~ sick and tired of people asking about
the recent break up with matt and A rumored
wedding?
what do you see in this picture? →

where do you work?

is pizza your favorite food?

is it possible to drive A stick shift in S.F.?

Are you experimenting with electronic drums?

to hell with your influences, what's A list
of stuff you're listening to lately?

Whos your favorite band?

Who?
NO. REAlly?
what do you think of the "Seattle Sound"?
HAve you heard the new Die Kreuzen album?

Are you planning on coming to seattle or its
surroundings areas to play a few show?
How many shows have you played in S.F. or its surrounding area?
Whats the crowd response?

Do you think that the Album Gluey porch Treatments
Actually exists or maybe there were only 15
Printed up?

I think the Album would sound even heavier on
A dance club sub woofer sound system in A
Euro Disco fag bar.
what do you think?

What really cool toys do you have?

do you think born Again is A good BLACK SABBATH Album?

did you know that C/Z is Collaborating with TOXIC SHOCK
& they have An Add in some fanzines and Amongst others Bands
Your 7"inch is listed?

wouldnt it be nice to walk into A store And
Find A Melvins Record?

Are your song writing styles changing in any WAY? or can we expect the same product forever from the melvins?

I didn't think so.

Tell me a story:

Now you Ask me A question And I will Respond with this

Thanks for the interview
We hope to see you sometime
cheeri-o

Dale,

Kenichewah,

OKAY, I have not lost my soulful, imbeded roots
as an honorary punk Rock, hard, heavy, Gunka Gunka
Gunka music slut. Nor have I been sucking up
the cute, innocent and clean image Olympia has to
offer either, but I have learned to appreciate some
of this Calvin/simplistic stuff enough to do my own
rendition, which is actually something I've been planning
on doing for years, so it's not really a rip off or
a ~~borrowed~~ borrowed influence. I'm making up excuses
because I don't think you'll like it, but I sent you
it anyhow just to fill up space, ~~cause~~ for I don't
have much new music to let you hear. So anyways..
"How the Hell ARE you doing dale Crover master of DRums?"

Send me boom box stuff NOW! I don't think too
many people will think you guys will suck, like you said
the legworshipping whores might", but B. F. D!

Chris and I were wandering around the campus one
Saturday evening, and we came across this band
playing. Inside we found 3 greeners jamming
on bad psychedellic blues, because thats what Greeners
do on Saturday evenings. They showed us their new
$200.00 worthless whammy pieces of shit KRamers
& New Laney Amps, I wasn't impressed. And then
over in the corner I noticed a left handed late 60's
fender mustang. After swallowing my puke I calmly
asked if they wanted to sell it and they said...
" Oh that old piece of shit?" "I dont care $50 bucks".
Chris entered the conversation and said.
"I dont know man it's pretty Junky." "OK twenty
bucks. it's only pawn shop material anyways. It's
nothing compared to our new Kramers.

63

So Chris and I Ran blindly through a ~~B~~ thick forest towards the light and to the van and to a bank machine and bought the pre CBS "65" left handed fender mustang. The END

My amp blew up. I got 2 more evel knievel motorcycles. <u>Rapeman</u>. Rapeman! Rapeman! I don't have any of their stuff on tape yet. probably because they don't have anything out. ~~but~~ but Rapeman are Steve Albini on guitar/vocals (from Big Black) & the drummer & bassplayer from Scratch Acid. I saw them last weekend and I think they are one of my favorite bands. I'll have to wait until I hear them on record. but god damn they were fucking cool live!

I defrosted the icebox with a hammer.
hours later Tracy noticed an awfully powerful fume & so we thought it was Free-on so we got the animals outside & the fumes became so bad that we couldn't go in the apt at all. it started to burn our skin & so we stayed next door for 1 night & in Tacoma the 2nd night & turns out it wasn't free on but even more of a deadly gas called sulfer dioxide. It's like if you were to fill a bucket of Bleach & Ammonia & tie someones face to it. I left a butterscotch swiss miss pudding out over night & it turned Bright flourescent green. So don't beat on your ice box with a hammer.
I talked to Jesse again. He's not getting a divorce anymore, instead he's buying more credit cards.

Touch N Go   Scratch Acid
Demo   side of
                    NIRVANA
floyd the barber
Spank Thru
Hairspray Queen
~~Aero zeppelin~~
Mexican Seafood
BeesWAX
Beans
~~Paper cuts~~
Big Cheese
Love Buzz
Aeros Zeppelin
~~Paper Cuts~~
pen CAP chew
montage of heck

Listed Price/HR

BASIC TRACK PRODUCTIONS
8-Track $15/hr

will
call me
BACK in
A HALF
Hour

Tri West Recording
$15/hr 8 TRACK

BLACKwood Laird
8 track
michael Lord Prod.
16 Track Recording

10 AM **50** BUCKS OR TAPE
SAT SUN
04   16   17   All day 9:00
3:00

3 hrs mix

how much per Hour for a 3 piece band

weekends this month
About 10 hours
evening
6-10 10
16 17

24   31

40 min material
half overdubs Guitar vocals

engineer?
Located?

I want to do a master for a pressing

american music
APex
half inch Reel Reel

So. side seattle
SEA TAC Airport
21040 5th Ave So. Seattle

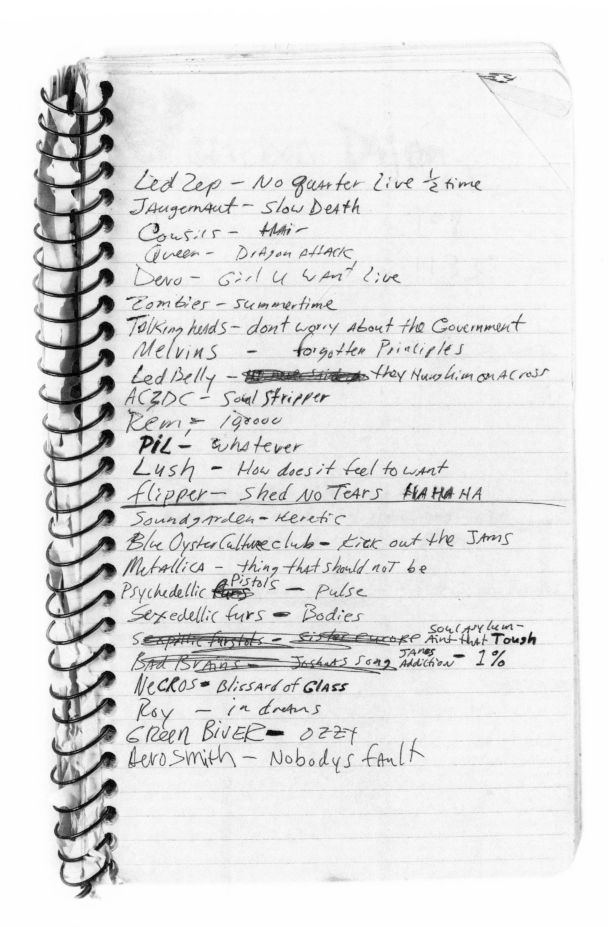

Led Zep — No quarter live ½ time
JAugemant — Slow Death
Cousins — hair
Queen — Dragon attack
Devo — Girl u want live
Zombies — summertime
Talking heads — dont worry About the Government
Melvins — forgotten Principles
Led Belly — ~~till the slide~~ they Hung him on A cross
AC/DC — Sical Stripper
Rem, 1980000
PiL — whatever
Lush — How does it feel to want
flipper — Shed No Tears HAHAHA
Soundgarden — Heretic
Blue Oyster Culture club — kick out the Jams
Metallica — thing that should not be
Psychedellic ~~furs~~ Pistols — Pulse
Sexedellic furs — Bodies
~~Sexadellic furstols~~ — ~~Sister Europe~~ Soul Asylum — Aint that Tough
~~Bad Brains~~ — ~~Joshuas Song~~ James Addiction — 1%
Necros — Blissard of Glass
Roy — in dreams
GReen RiveR — Ozzy
AeroSmith — Nobodys fault

Bitching About Prog-Rock

Ing lots of Ings. Descriptive words
end IN INg. like masturbating, over exagerating
~~exagerating~~. munching, chewing hot stacked-
earth momma sitting in the open woods of
Nottingham early in the mornings fog. listening
to Stairway to Heaven while stringing beads. Not
applying makeup. In tune, Aqua man circles
emulating from a forehead. Bouncing off of a crystal
necklace. A neck strangled by piano wire.
"I have friends both on land and in the sky".
But the sea Mr French? "I dog paddle for I am
now a teeny little goblin-dancing-pixie-
-Zamphire master of the pan flute."
    Sold over a zillion archery dummies in Europe
alone! The dummys are sex dolls stuffed with
leaches & a substance of Ginger Root, penny Royal
tea, Ginseng, B-vitamins, sweet cut-grass
and a spoiled pound of ground baby veal (Lamb.)
    Doctor Bronner claims! Apply the archery
Dummy-substance naked in the forest. Dilute!
Dilute! Mr Merlin. Dilute! Dilute!
sprinkling minute metal shavings into the eyes of
a praised cult ~~figure~~. A male.
Here now in the woods. Getting back to Nature.
The breath is visible as he exhales from
the bull-like nostrils. scraping back leg
into the ground. mounting the earth momma.
no matter how hard you try, sex will always
Resurface.
    Buffy and Jody get it on. Rick Wakeman
does the soundtrack.

Hi   first of all I enjoy your show.

Jesse Helms is a dirty homosexual.
The Imperial wizard of the KKK is a nigger.
~~with thee harsh words of a sweet or sour~~
~~Bitter beer batter~~ grease splatter ~~scatter.~~
~~Mad Hatter.~~

~~Do you like the show~~
Am I guilty of such hipness?
No longer is there hipness or such Tom foolery
for this boy whos name is ~~████~~. Hi that is my
name. I was thinking thee other day.
of my name and ~~thought~~ I would write you
NOT in regards to my name regardless of thee
sentence which may have thrown you off.
~~or got you off.~~ I could only be such a
fool to modestly think ~~so it's Lord coould~~
~~think~~   How could one ˢᵘᶜʰ suck winding-force
of so many celebs colon; in hopes of
~~C████ for~~ celebrating the calibre of
such hipness. May I throw out my hip?
I had a bad fall. I limped.
I limped with the best of them.
I have now come to the conclusion
that I have been ●● confused for many
days and I now love many days and
many many of those ᴵ ˡᵒᵛᵉ whom I have
so wrongly accused of being hip.
Those who come to celebrate with one
another only for the reasons of
companionship in which they so
Rightly share. They share the
same things. They seek out
others. So fuck.
At peace am I ~~████████~~ you're a good one.

"MONTE VISTA" SO TACOMA WAY

The name even reakes of suburban subdivision Hell. I walked into the place to buy a patch cord. After I bought it I noticed a bunch of amps behind a sliding glass door. There were new Peavys marshalls Fenders. After Gawking at the list price I checked out the used amps. I noticed an old Fender. It's the kind thats about four Feet tall and has SIX tens in it. It's basically a twin reverb. So I closed the door, plused in the ~~old~~ cheap Peavey tryout gee-tar And Fucked around with the reverb & tremolo. It Sounded pretty cool kind of like the cramps. Shit it was only $200.00, ~~It~~ kind of beat, so I was interested. ~~It's~~ Fuck it, I cranked it up way loud to see what kind of balls it had. Right then mr. Suavo Coolo ~~Friend~~ Frienly o store dude walked in and turned it down. ~~A~~ He had a shit eating grin on and said "Jams eh".
I said "Yeah man.

71

"Can I put this on Lay-a-way"
He said "Sure $20 bucks down
15 bucks a week for ninety
days." "Far out" He went away
so I cranked it again, so he
walks back in with his diahareha
smile and turns it down.
What a dick I should have
thrown it threw the godamn
sliding glass door. I said
sheeeatt! I left. That old
Fuckin fender would a blew any
way.

Globetrotters theme
Lucy in the Sky - william shatner
The sensitive little boy - ^{pro}GAY Record
Pusherman - superfly sndtrk
Shes got you - Patsy Cline
frustrated - Chipmunk punk (Knack)
Keep yer hands off her - leadbelly
   JAVA - floyd Cramer
   In love ⟩ Marine Girls
   Honey

mollys lips - vaselines
Ballad of Evel Knievel
Somethin like that - NWA
TV Girl - Beat Happening
Scratchit out ⟩ Go team (Tam sings)
Bikini twilight ⟩ me & Calvin & Toby
He never said a mumblen word - Leadbelly

73

Telly SAVALAS greasing up his head and ramming it
in and out! IN and out of another TV personalities.
ass. who's ass? who cares. either way it's a
cheap way to get an immediate laugh.
← put the stars name here.
It could be even more affective if it is a male.
Homosexual scandals amongst celebrities are always a
shure fire chuckle getter.

How about Goober and Gomer givin it to each other.
or Gary coleman (Arnold on different stokes) and
emanuelle lewis (Webster) veesus monkey love in
the 69 tongue-butt position.   Why am I
so Sexually concious? why can I not be
clone Have I had too many porns? or Charles
Bukowski? Is this the easy way out?
NO. Sex is dirty. It is over rated.
"I don't want to be touched after its over."
"It wasn't worth it to cheat on my partner."
   It took him 3 days to realize why he was
depressed.   After all, his male friends
approved with smurks and trumpeting farts.
Besides tellys stubble scratched the inner walls of
my colon.   Do not be fooled by shiny,
   waxy   baldness.   His neck was a
JACK HAMMER. Very talented.   Shecky Greene
Joined in.   We ran up a huge gold card
Bill.   Thats Alright, I'm a high roller.
   All my celebrity friends are here with me.
Here in Las Vegas. Naked, shaved and greased.
These life size card board cut-outs store away easily in my
closet.   Lolli pop up you know where.
   Lolli lolli lolli pop.

OH I'm so damn proud of ~~them~~. you ~~~~
A Triumphant victory for mankind. MAybe there
is Hope. ~~~~ It brought a tear to
& A lump in my throat
my eye. Staring out the window in A traffic JAm
for 3 hours watching the little lawnmower cars zoom
past hundreds of Happy Westerners, receiving them
with a compassionate, full contact smile and stare. You've
made it. Have some fruit. Now you too can purchase
pastel bed sheets, Electronics And toilet paper of
your ~~~~ wildest dreams. You have so much to learn.
Thousands of Grown infants, Rosy red cheeks ~~~~
fully dressed in Acid wash pants & Jackets,
males with moustache, Ladies with permanent hair.
Look over there! it's my mom. She ~~~~ is
so many years more advanced in the Art of shopping &
matching outfits from the luxury of selection.
You have so much to learn. Rock And Roll has
now just begun. Don't hide the products
you have bought under your seats. prepare yourself
for A full Search as you enter back through the
border. Take note of the leaflets And flyers
~~~~ on your windshield informing you
And legal representation
where to Acquire credit. I'm happy for you.
please Reproduce. We're doing All we can
over here As well.

groon

APly
APPly
Slowly, steadily and righteously
walk you
through the
mysterious
world of
fashion

Laydown your WARM babies on my cold feet
At the end of my Bed and then

I Apologize for Apologizing and drink
the poison in me then the roof cooked

Taste buds soak Absorbant sponge water and
my tongue Runs Across the roof of my mouth
and it feels like A small Rib cage
Giant Nose Hair Booger Hinge

I don't mind my captivity, but the pelt
and habitat description on the bottle
next to the cage is A bit disfasteful,
Fucking Bull HAd A vision, He would write A
PUNK ROCK operA

THE STORY

his name is forest And he is the one
who put's CALcium in the Tab soft drinks.
and his followers wave their Arms in unison
with his. Clenching crimping irons And
MAscArA (black), "We must make the woods
Pretty AgAin"), shouted the steam engine inventor.
    Yes but what About the Piles of MAsses?
the Heaping mounds of sponge, severed Pore,
And Taste bud chunks. nervously bitten and
SPAT out of the mouth from the Chiwawa
Head, Johnny MAthis monster? asked chowder.)
    It is sucking dry All the resin from the
Bong WAter River. I sAy we destroy the filter
WAlls. (shouted Helium Boy.) And then (fucking) SPoke..
                                    (Bull)

Skip 2 pages
And go on →

He spat Dark brown bubbling snoose from the dried veins of New Age believers. it soaked into the ground instantly which Reminded him that the woods are in greater need of emergency than he thought. he said "look my friends, spit and see the Quickness of the soil.

And As all 5 beings spat and observed, Tony Defranco crabs surfaced and gobbled what little moisture they could before being stepped on and crushed and Quickly consumed by our hero's. the feast was celebrated with an offering of spam fresh squeezed grease pockets of spam and pepperoni chunks filled to the Rim of an ancient 1990's Teenage unwanted baby skull.

But this does not explain our misfortune Grunted Buttchowder. Please, please tell us more Fucking Bull and so Fucking Bull spoke again.

It was in my vision that I saw stoners destroy a church with No Roof and only 3 walls. and there were candles, many candles and the Virgin Mary Hooked thru her back on a meat Hook, and one of the male stoners said "Dude Hooker headers!" then stopped dead in his tracks with his hand just softly touching her firm breast and noticed how Painfully Beautiful she was, how pure, and white, how peaceful wrapped in chicken and barbed wire with a not yet

ON All <u>drums</u> - get rid of Hi HAT Hiss.

<u>Downer</u> - Re-Do All Vocals & get someone with A
Deep voice to repeat solo vocals in monotone
~~Dub extra~~ Re-Do All Guitar & bass

<u>floyd</u> - Re-Do bass - Dub extra Guitar

<u>Paper Cuts</u> - Dub Guitar - Dub Singing Harmony
~~bass~~ Re-Do Bass

<u>Spank thru</u> - Re-Do Bass

~~[scribbled out]~~

<u>Hairspray Queen</u> - Re-Do everything

<u>Pen Cap chew</u> - Re·Do everything

<u>Mexican Seafood</u> - Re - D① Guitar Drums Voc.
(Dales drums)

<u>ERecTum</u>

Love Buzz Bigcheese ERECTum weirdo
Bees WAX Aeroszeppelin Vendetagainst
Annoveyourcist

A finished Anarchy sign spray painted on her Robe.
Then his head turned slowly to his mates, ~~And~~
~~cried~~ A trickle of Teardrop Rolled down his
ugly fucking zitted out face and cried:
"This is WRONG! We MUST STOP This"!
   and so One of the girl stoners kind of put all her
weight on one foot And stuck her acid wash ASS out,
~~held A cigarette~~ took a big drag off of a lucky STRIKE
cigarette, gave a very cool blank/stoned expression
under those heavily eye shadow (Blue) thicker than
snot lashed eyes, exhaled and in a groggy dry
wheezing, charred lung voice said, "So whAT were
bored." And the others immediately Ran around
screaming, wooo Hooo (in that ~~t~~One of voice
that says "I'm very drunk, excited and A total
idiot"!) they smashed and Burned and SPRAYED
BlAck, flag, DRI ~~×~~ as well as Dokken and
Whitesnake. Then guess whAT? asked fucking Bull,
~~they added A shite they got Bored and~~
~~went AWAY~~ WHAT? WHAT happened shit
Butt chowder? fucking Bull said: ~~A~~ After
Awhile they became bored with vandalizing
the church And went ~~to~~ AWAY to buy a gram.
So I suggest we all just connect our vitals
to this ancient cow milking HookAH
And Relax, because the River will never dry
up for it is fed by the mountains which
will Always be Addicted to boredom.

               The END

Fear - We gotta getoutta this place
Gary Numan - It must have been years
PIL - Annalisa
Elvis Costello - Pump it up
Pop o pies - I Am the Walrus
Tales of Terror - Chambers of Horror

BRing

SNARE

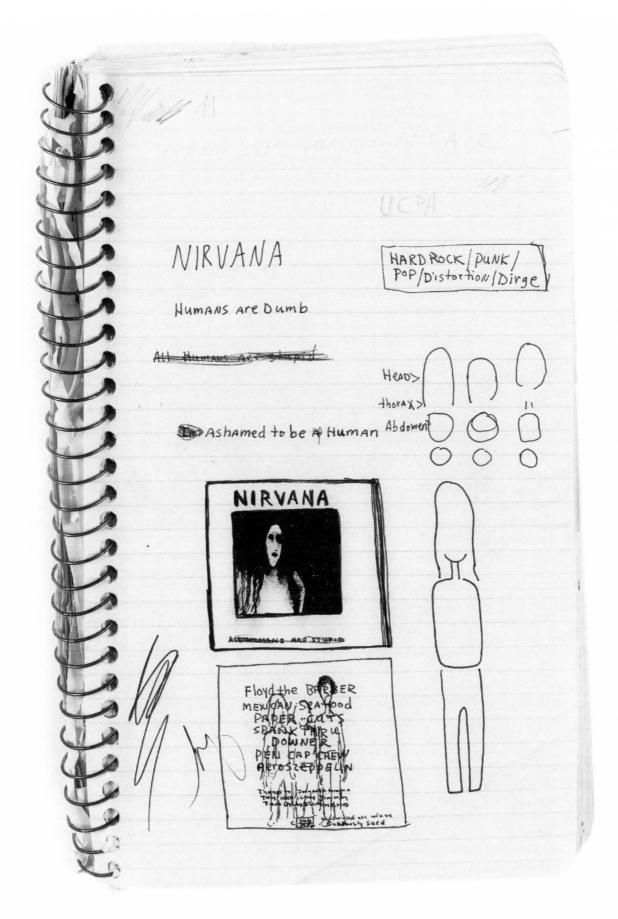

NIRVANA

HARD ROCK / PUNK / POP / Distortion / Dirge

Humans are Dumb

~~All Humans Are stupid~~

Head>

thorax>

Abdomen

~~I'm~~ Ashamed to be A Human

NIRVANA

ALL HUMANS ARE STUPID

Floyd the BARBER
MEXICAN SEAFOOD
PAPER CUTS
SPANK THRU
DOWNER
PEN CAP CHEW
AEROSZEPPELIN

Critic goes GOD

The first thing i did WAS burn All
my CharLes Bukowski books. I
got the tinfoil out and spread it
on the floor, Ripped the ~~books~~
filthy innards of plankton-literature
into small pieces, and struck A
match. ITurned out the lights And
watched the flames Along with some
home Super 8 movies I had made
while under the influence of this life
I've decided to change.   The movies
were typical Gore slash shit Along with
puppets fucking, oh And the psychic TV-
~~radiance~~-like effect of ArTy subjects
turning And floating ~~about~~ in A meaningful
surrealistic sense. bullshit, it was
like watching A Real estate seminar, but
it set A nice background for my MTV
Direction towards god.   God. God.
God. Im Crosslegged, Rosary to
~~my Right,   Bible to my left.~~ the left
of me, Bible to the Right, here I Am
Stuck in the middle with you". stuck in the
middle with you.' who Sang that song?
AtlantA Rhythm Section? steve miller,
UM, God. 'ATlantA Rhythm Section
hAs the dorkiest looking members, that
one Guy with GreAsy pig fat hAir, And
BlacK Rimmed Glasses. But the

Stupidest looking 70's Rock star has to
be that one Guy in Slade, the fucker-
Cut his bangs so high up on his forehead.
"He looks like Woody from the bay City
Rollers". I know this kid in Aberdeen
who looks exactly like woody. Jesus you
wouldn't believe it, the same teeth and
nose, ~~it's not sad it's just funny~~
I would love to look like woody, then
I could start my band and ~~never~~ play
Saturday Night. "Was kiss on
Saturday Night live? Naw ~~the co~~ they
couldn't have, ~~people~~ fans would have trashed
the studio & beat up Don Pardo, ~~and
Raped Lorraine Newman~~. I would love
to be those kids on the back of kiss
Alive, the ones holding the banner.
Kiss. I don't even like kiss.
    Rock Trivia. God im so sick
of Rock Trivia, big deal it's like
what am i gonna do when I'm old,
if i Already know everything About
Rock'n Roll by the time im 19?
    God only knows ~~now adays~~ there's
no facts to be learned About All these
worthless Rip off Nostalgic bands. of the 80's.
    Oh yeah i decided to eventually
become An H Addict And slowly decay
on the streets of Idaho. or some

middle of the road ⬛ state like that.
I'll be so bored that ill just read
About what I lived thru And purposely
stayed Naive, because you mR Rock
Critic Are gonna be Bored when your old.
Bored Bored Bored. So Am I so Are
old people today, I don't wANt A
GrAnd daughter of mine chAnging my soiled
Rubber underwear while f And sucking on Ry-Krisp,
Clinging to existence just so I cAn
reminice About my life As A professional
Remeniscent. Besides, my memory
is Already shot, from too much Pot
smoking A few years back. I saw
these Hippies on the merve Griffin show
claiming they had NASAl SPRAys wich
would increase youre memory, I Also
SAw this couple who swore, with the
proper trAining," you cAN have up to 10
orgAsms before ejAculAting, sure
if you tie A rubber bAnd to the end.
        All this wonderfully important
deep thought hindered me from REAlizing
that the entire House WAS filled
with smoke from the ChArles Bukowski
Books, And A very nice sized flame
had spread to the curtains, which Alarmed
me I had only A few minutes to
get out of the House, so much for God.

Sexually Transmitted Diseases
in the espresso At the Smithfield

Green RiveR — Aint Nothin to do
Dead Boys — Dead River Boys
Dicks — Police force
Clown Alley — on the way up
Vox Pop — Production
SKIN DIVER — αD NO. 7
Shock'n Blue — HoT SAND
Bangles — HAZy shade of Winter
the eyes — Dont tAlk to me
Saccharine Trust — Peace frog
~~Youre~~ Big Dipper — Youre NoT PAtsy
Big BLACK — CRACK uP
Big Boys — A Political
Alice Cooper — Muscle of Love
GReg SAge — StRAight AHeAD
MAlfunkshun — Stars And You

SMelvins —
                    smell my Finger

Devo — TURN AROUND

White Zombie — RATmouth
Zombies — Time of the SEASON
DICKS — off Duty SAilor
A PARt of the Tape that will be FAst forwarded every time its played
The Tonsil Song HA HA HA HA HA HA HA HAHA

ELVIS
Cooper

Aneurysm

Come on over & do the twist

over do it & have a fit

Come on over & shoot the shit

I love you so much it makes me
        sick

she keeps it pumpin straight to my heart

SAPPY

And if you save yourself
you will - think your happy
Hell keep you in A JAr
then youll - think your happy
Hell give you breather Holes
then youll - think your happy
Hell cover you in grASs
then youll - think your happy now

(Your in A CAUNDRY ROOM)
conclusion came to you AM

And if you HEAL yourself
you will make Him happy
youll WALLow in your shit

And if you cure yourself

88

Verse Chorus Verse

Neither side is sacred ~~there's no room~~ *no one wants* to win
Feeling so sedated think I'll just give in
Takin medication till our stomachs ~~full~~
wouldn't wanna ~~fake~~ it — if I had a soul

The grass is greener over here
your the fog that keeps me clear
your the reason I feel pain

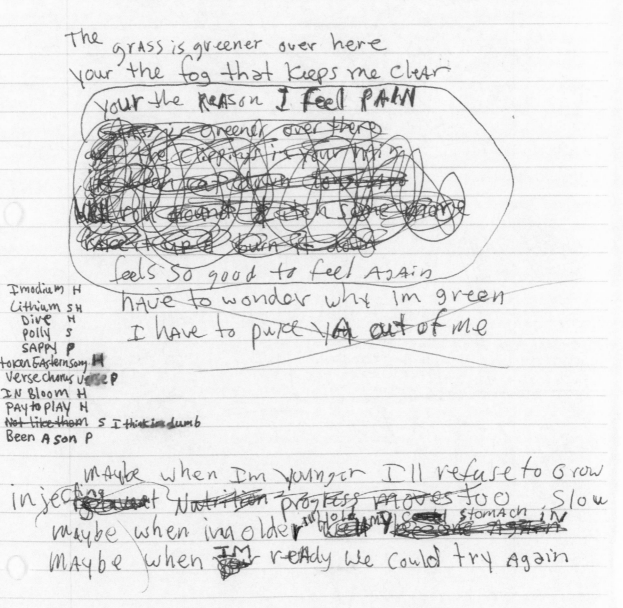

feels so good to feel again
have to wonder why im green
I have to purge ya out of me

Imodium H
Lithium S H
Dive H
Polly S
Sappy P
token Eastern song H
Verse chorus verse P
In Bloom H
Pay to Play H
~~Not like them~~ S I think im dumb
Been A son P

Maybe when Im younger I'll refuse to grow
injecting ~~~~ ~~Nutrition~~ progress moves too slow
maybe when im older ~~~~ stomach in
Maybe when Im ready we could try again

Dive

Pick me - pick me YEAH
Let A low long signal
At ease   At least YEAH
everyone is Hollow
Pick me — Pick me YEAH
everyone is WAiting
Pick me - Pick me YEAH
~~you will~~ even pay them
You CAN
           Hey
       Dive Dive Dive Dive in me

Kiss this kiss that YEAH
let A low long signal
At ease Atease YEAH
You CAN be my Hero
Pick me pick me yeAH
everyone is ~~waiting Hollow~~ WAiting
Hit me Hit me yeah
~~Decan even swallow~~
I'm real good At Hating

91

Hi Eugene,

I'm staying at a friends house here in Olympia listening to a crappy college radio show. I've realized that it's not because there are no good bands but because the DJs have Bloody awful taste in music. OH yes, and to prove my point, right now theyre playing a ~~xxxx~~ NIRVANA song from an old Demo.

How's Captain America? I hear we're playing some shows together when we go over to England. I can't wait! Were really looking forward to it. all our friends will be there at Redding. Mudhoney Babes in Toyland, sonic youth, L7, etc. Ashure blow out!

well, we won the war.

Patriotic Propaganda is in full effect. we have the privilege of purchasing Desert Storm trading cards, flags, bumperstic, and many video versions of our triumphant victory. When I walk down the street I feel like i'm at a Nuremburg rally.

Hey, maybe Nirvana & Captain America could go on tour together in the states and burn American flags on stage. we'll be going out again in Sept If youre interested, I'll keep you posted. well heres the live Mollys lips 7" I find it embarrasing because it's just simply a bad version. but it was a great privilege to play one of your songs and to play together at a show and to meet you all. It was easily the

(GREATEST Moment of my) Li

The Vaselines have been my favorite H /
band for a long while now and and
Geez. I cant wait to see you all
soon and thanks for writing.

(and my (Jim's) I got evicted from my apt. I'm living in
my car so I have no address but here's
chris's phone number for messages

your pal kurdt

Derek

1 Stooges — Raw power
2 Beatles — ~~meet the Beatles~~ Something new
3. Leadbellys last sessions
4 Scratch Acid — 1st EP
5. Butthole surfers — 1st EP
6. Vaselines — 1st EP
7. Fang — Land Shark
8 Smithereens — especially for you
9 Tales of terror — tales of terror
10. Pixies — Surfer Rosa
11. Mudhoney — Super fuzz Bigmuff
12. Flipper — Generic flipper
13. Black flag — my WAR
14 Black Sabbath — master of Reality
15. Credence Clearwater — Bayou
16 Blue cheer — Vincebus eruptum
17. The knack — Get the knack
18. Saccharin trust — 1st EP
19. Roy Orbison — Greatest hits
20 Gang of four — Entertainment
21. Wipers   — ~~Youth of America~~ is this real
22. Shocking Blue — shocking Blue
23. Bad brains — Rock for Light
24. Best Happening — Jamboree
25. Aerosmith — Rocks
26. Shonen Knife — ks cassette burning farm
27. Young marble Giants — ymg
28. Velvet underground — white light white heat
29. Sex pistols — never mind the Bollocks

- ☐   I am threatened by ridicule
- ☐ I am overly concience of ~~So~~ the sincerity i~~n~~ my voice.
- ☐ I like to have sex with ~~a~~ people
- ☐ I love my parents ~~yet~~ I disagree with merely everything they stand for.
- ☐ I understand and appreciate the ~~value of~~ religion for ~~some people~~ others.
- ☐ my emotions are affected by music.
  -     punk rock means freedom
- ☐ I use bits and pieces of others personalities to form my own.
- ☐
- ☐
- ☐

Hi, I like punk rock more than anything in the whole wide world. and so I thought I'd would xerox words on paper & staple them together and sell them to punk Rockers & others who don't know much about punk Rock and for those who don't care or who don't deserve the privilege and also to those who are <u>Bored</u> with it.

    I Also don't know very much About punk Rock

As far as the History is concerned Well, me too. I'm bored or just uninspired. maybe were just takin a break, a rest or recovery from Hardcore. I never really liked hardcore, mainly because it was too macho and there were so many intimidating rules. I remember when I first started hanging out with friends who were a few months more advanced in proper punk rock lingo & etiquette, I said, "hey lets listen to some punk" and this guy said "man its not called punk anymore its called HARD CORE! Gee, I felt like a heel. HARD CORE was an obvious mutation of 77 punk because punk popularity reached the suburbs and then all of a sudden jocks who already had short hair from the wrestling team got involved because

[left margin:] As far as the History is concerned But I ~~do know~~ do ~~know~~ HAVE AN opinion ~~of~~ on WHAT PUNK ROCK means to me. it means Freedom from...

96

it was supposedly an easy energy release and
an excuse to fight. I could probably
explain why I never liked hardcore in
a million different ways but lets just
say it wasn't my cup of TEA. All you
have to do is read the letter section
from MAXimum Rock-n-Roll from the
pAst 6 years and you may understand
what I mean.

Dispensable as recycled toilet tissue, they breed like rabbits and their hands will be sent back attached to key chains. If Jimmi Hendrix were alive he would more than likely have a long back (bi level) hair cut and slick, sequin threads sporting a new Aero dynamic-90's guitar with zebra stripes and a pointy headstock. Iggy pop at a recent gig in L.A. Jammed with slash from Guns-n-roses on a 20 minute rendition of louie louie.

The journalist left a red ~~circle~~ circle, imprint from the camera lens on the forehead of a mother who has 5 sons in the persian gulf. She was asked to describe just exactly how she feels of this situation while holding her sons ~~her sons~~ military portraits in her lap. A student listening to old R.E.M watches the mother on T.V. and becomes exited by the idea that has just burst from his environmentally & socially ~~deprived~~ mind; "maybe there will be reason now for A REVOLUTION!

I like following the rise of entertainers careers while they still ~~haven't to~~ make it, ~~while in~~ ~~their early to late twenties~~. I like to know everything about them, and if enough information isn't available, then tabloids will be sufficient. I like punk rock. I like girls with weird eyes. I like drugs. I like passion. I like things that are built well. I like innocence. I like and am grateful for the blue collar worker whos existence allows Artists to not have to work at ~~menial~~ menial jobs. I like killing gluttony. I like playing my cards wrong.

But my Body And mind wont Allow me to TAKE them

I like various styles of music. I like making
fun of musicians whom I feel pladgerise or
offend music as art by exploiting pushing their
embarrasingly, pathetic versions of their work.
I like to write poetry. I like to ignore other's onto
poetry. I like vinyl. I like nature and animals. the public
I like to swim. I like to be with my friends.
I like to be by myself. I like to feel guilty
for being a white, American male.
I love to sleep. I like to fill my mouth
with seeds and spit them out at random
as I walk. I like to taunt small, barking
dogs in parked cars. I like to make people feel
happy and superior in their reaction towards
my appearance. I like to feel predjudice
towards people who are predjudice. I like
to make incisions into the belly of infants then
fuck the incisions until the child dies.
    I like to dream that someday we will have
a sense of Generational Solidarity amongst the
youth of the world. I like to make insidious
efforts to Avoid Conflict. I like to have
strong opinions with nothing to back them up
with besides MY PRIMAL sincerity.
    I like sincerity. I LACK sincerity.
these are not opinions. these are not words of wisdom,
this is a disclaimer. a disclaimer for my
lack of education, for my loss of inspiration,
for my unnerving quest for affection and
my perfunctory shamefullnes or towards many who
are of my relative age. Its not even A
Poem. its Just A Big pile of shit. like ME.

I like to complain and do nothing to make things better. I like to blame my parents generation for coming so close to social ~~total~~ change. then giving up after a few successful ~~efforts~~ by the media & Government ~~to~~ deface the movement by ~~accusing~~ using the mansons ~~as~~ and other Hippie representatives as ~~examples~~ propaganda examples on how they were nothing but unpatriotic, communist, satanic, inhuman diseases. and in turn the baby boomers become the ultimate, conforming, yuppie hypocrites a generation has ever produced.

I like to calmly and rationally discuss my views in a conformist manor even though I consider myself to the extreme left.
I like to infiltrate the mechanics of a system by posing as one of them, then slowly start the rot from the inside of the empire.
I like to ~~assassinate~~ ASSAsinate the lesser & greater of two evils.
I like to impeach God.
I like to Abort christ.

natural less violent

I like to fuck sheep.
I like the comfort in knowing that women are ~~generally~~ superior, ~~and naturally~~ and naturally less violent than men.
I like the comfort in knowing that women are the only future in rock and roll.

I like the comfort in knowing that the
Afro American invented Rock and roll
yet has only been rewarded, or awarded
for their accomplishments when conforming
to the white mans standards.
   I like the comfort in knowing that the
Afro American has once again been the
only race that HAS brought a new form
of original music to this decade! hip hop/rAp.

censorship is VERY AmericAN.

I have met many minds able to store and translate
a pregnantly large amound of information, yet
they haven't an ounce of talent for wisdom or
the appreciation Of passion.

The conspiracy to success in America (uhmericuh)
is immediacy. To expose in great repetition to the minds of
small attention spans. fast, speedy, Now with even more
NAcho cheese flavor! here today, gone tomorrow because
yesterdays following WAS nothing more than a tool in every
individuals need for self importance, entertainment and
social rituals. Art that has long lasting vAlue cannot
be appreciated by majorities, only the
same, small percent will appreciate vAlue ARTs patience
tips   as they always have. this is good. the ones
      who are unaware do not deserve false suggestions
   in their purchasing duties.

~~music has absolutely nothing to do with a~~
~~musicians personal beliefs, its not an extention~~
~~of personality or a story before caused~~
~~as feeling before~~

Scenarios revolve. Verbal communication is
exhausted. sit coms are scenarios and so
is our conversation. ~~to gather~~
~~for a party to gather to~~

our party gathers ~~to congregate to~~ out of boredom.
role playing for affection & acceptance and
to disinfect nagging germs ending in silence,
and accomplishment-produced violations
on those who werent here to play.
    they were invited, maybe in a museum
far from now.
I Am now ~~so~~ in my sad stage, before it
was naive hate. I want to be the first
to discover and discard before its
popularity. Tomorrow the I wont care
    stage is predicted, and im not looking
forward to it. maybe vegetables will
diffuse the chemicals ~~which produce~~
i produce inside me, an easy excuse,
(these chemicals.) I rarely ~~sdlpoa~~ use
my instrument. it used to be so exciting.
working on music is not a chore. It's now
a waste of time to practice. Every
other month I buy the results from
the Air.
Ask not what you can do to your rock stAr.

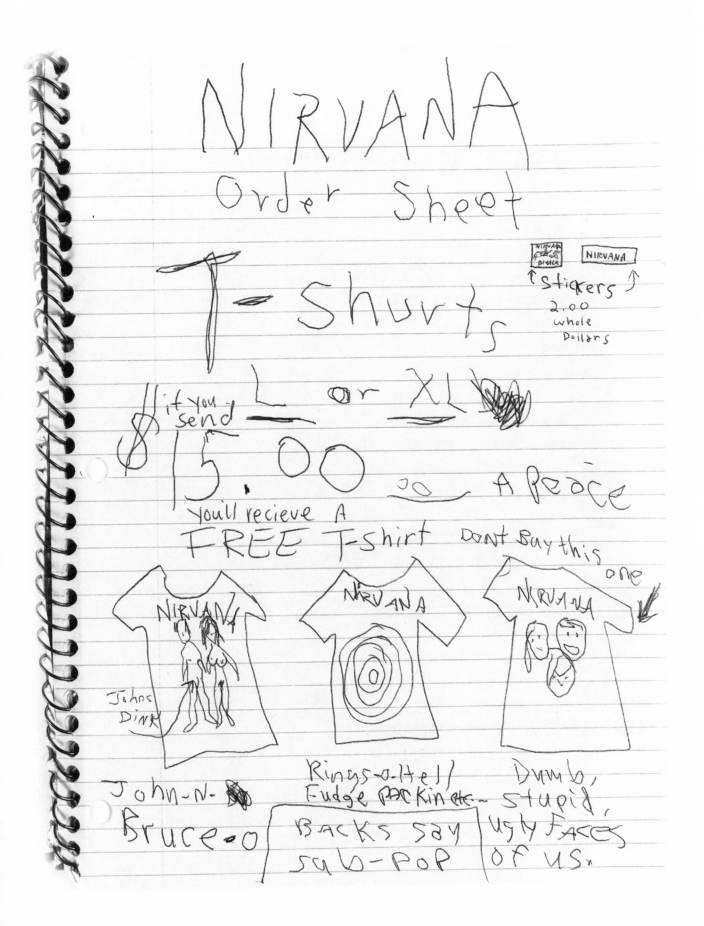

NIRVANA
Order Sheet

T-Shurts

NIRVANA | NIRVANA
↑ Stickers ↑
2.00
whole
Dollars

if you send L or XL

$15.00 ⚬⚬ A Peace

You'll recieve A
FREE T-shirt   Don't Buy this one

NIRVANA   NIRVANA   NIRVANA

Johns
Dink

John-N-   Rings-o-Hell   Dumb,
Bruce-o   Fudge packin etc   stupid,
            Backs say   ugly Faces
            sab-pop   of us.

103

~~≈≈≈≈≈≈≈≈≈≈≈≈≈≈≈≈≈≈≈≈≈~~

A manic depressive on smack floating in A WARm ~~a~~ deprevAtion tank, singing leonard cohen, masturbating, watching golfers fish while dreaming of ~~A~~ stamp Collection.

~~≈≈≈≈≈≈≈≈≈≈≈≈≈≈≈≈≈≈~~

the king of words is: EVERYthing

I can only ~~fuck~~ and **Sing**.
HAve you ever felt like you cared so much that you wanted to kill ~~≈≈≈≈~~ your GermS?

who will be the King and Queen of the outcasts?

I've lost my **MIND** many times, and my wallet many more.
IN the Simplest terms:

~~≈≈≈≈≈≈≈≈≈≈≈≈≈≈≈≈~~

1 Dont RApe
2 Dont be predjudice
3 Dont be Sexist
~~≈≈≈≈≈≈≈≈≈≈≈≈≈≈≈≈≈~~
4 Love your children
5 Love your Neighbor
6 Love yourself
Don't let your opinions obstruct the Aforementioned list

I was about 13 and going through the common ~~not quite puberty~~ pre pubescent, hate your parents, wish you could still play with dolls but instead, feel unusually weird around Girls-syndrome.

I was a rodent-like, underdeveloped, hyperactive spaz who could fit his entire torsoe in one leg of his bell bottomed jeans, and I was frustrated, I needed to let off some steam.

I went to the movies with my friends.

We saw "over the Edge."

Over the edge is a ~~movie~~ story of troubled youth, vandalism, parental negligence, and most importantly ~~real estate~~ real estate development dysfunctional families

Its true in a sense that you can make a comfortable living at it — ~~but other than that its not interesting too~~ operating of a profession. But besides financial security it really isnt that wise of a profession. one of the main problems I have ~~because~~ I feel like im being evaluated 24 hrs a day, ~~being in a band~~ is hard work and the acclaim itself isnt worth it unless you still like playing And I do god how I do love playing live, its the most primal form of energy release you can share with other people besides having sex or taking drugs. So if you see A good live show on drugs and then later that evening have sex, youve basically covered all the bases of energy release, and we all need to let off steam, its easier and safer than protesting abortion clinics or praising God or wanting to hurt your Brother
        SO   go to A
            show dance around a bit
    and copulate

Primary

The second time we broke it off
I ~~lost~~ a voice sincerity was washed
I love myself better than you - I know its
wrong so what should I do?

Im on a plaine - I cant complain

The 18th time we broke it off
I heard a noise ~~so we~~ we ~~burnt~~ a cross
we walked hand in hand in our parade
~~we~~ took off our robes and began ~~to~~ rape

you stole things from me - All Apologies
I stole things from you - I will stand accused
what else can i do - I belong to you
what else can there be - All Apologies

what else can I say - All my words are grey
what else should I write? - I dont want to fight
how else could I feel? - All our lips are sealed
what do you expect? - Im a nervous wreck

in the sun in the sun i feel as one
in the sun in the **sun** Im married
                                        marriage
     yeah yeah yeah yeah

NOT Finished

I Think I'm Dumb

mollyslips slushy-VAselines

I'm not like them – but I can pretend
the sun is Gone – but I have A light
the dAy is done – but im hAving fun
I think im dumb – or maybe just happy

my heart is broke but I have some Glue
Help me inhale & mend it with you
well floAt Around & hang out on clouds
then we'll come down & hAve A hangover.

Skin the Sun & fall Asleep
breathe AWAY – the soul is weak
lesson learned – wish me luck
Soothe the burn – WAKe me up

I've been told that an artist is in need of
constant tragedy to fully express their work,
but I'm not an artist and when I say I
in a song, that doesn't neccesarily mean
that ~~that~~ person is me and it doesn't mean
im just a story teller, it means whoever
or whatever you want because everyone
has their own definition of specific words
and when your dealing in the context of
music you cant expect ~~universal meanings~~ *words.
to ~~have~~ the same ~~as~~ meaning ~~as in~~ everyday
use of our vocabulary because I consider music
art and when I say "that song is art"
I dont mean in comparison to A painting
because ~~If~~ the visual arts are not nearly
as sacred as the transcribed or Audio commun-
ications, but it is art and ~~these~~
~~our was a more tragic loss this~~
~~society this~~ somewhere I feel this society ~~and other~~
has lost its ~~most~~ valuable sense
of what art is, Art is expression.
in expression you need 100% full freedom
and our freedom to express our
art is seriously being fucked
with. FUCK, the word fuck has
as many connotations as does the
word Art and ~~Im cant~~ far beyond
the point of sitting down and casually
~~explaining about~~ complaining this problem to the
Right wing control freaks who Are
the main ~~defenders~~ offender of destroying

Art. I ⊘⊘⊘ wont calmly and Literally
complain to YOU! I'm going to fucking
Kill. I'm going to fucking
Destroy your MACHO, sAdistic,
Sick Right wing, religiously
Abusive opinions on how we
As A whole should operate
According to YOUR conditions.
before I die
many will die with me and they
will deserve it. see you
        IN Hell
                    love kuvdt
                        cobain

        thanks for the TRAgedy I need
        it for my Art.
    punk Rock is Art ~~the problem~~
      Punk Rock to me means freedom.
    the only problem ive had with the situAtionists
    ⊘ punk rock ethic is that Absolute denial
    ~~of~~ Anything ⊘ sacred, I find a ~~lot~~
    ~~few~~ things sacred ⊘⊘⊘ ~~like~~ Such as
    the superior ~~ty of~~ women and the negro
    ~~have and the things theyve~~ HAd ~~to~~ Contribute
    to ~~on~~ Art. I guess what im sAying is
    that Art is sAcred.
        punk rock is freedom
      expression And right to express is vital
    Anyone CAN be artistic.

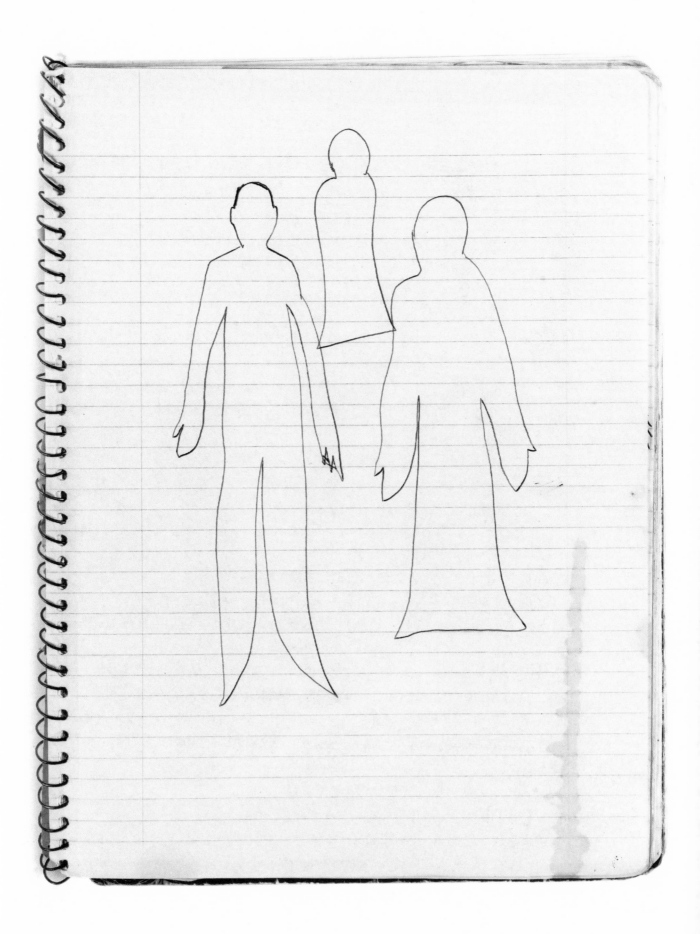

disparagement - Belittlement

I have a lot to say, but i'll leave that to
you, I'll leave that to those who have
the ability to **expound** their whines better than I.
The facts to back up the complaints
and the patience to debate, the
impossible deprogramming of the plantation
owners, and their workers and their slaves.
The slaves born into their world one
UN-questioning, and unaware through their
generations acceptance of "thats just the
way it is", stripped of culture in
the pen, bred in a pen and losing
ink, but refilling to pray of disposable
goods and pray of the dispensable through
the faith given by the feudal lords "take it or leave it."
impulse "like it or lump it." "I brought you into this
world and ill take you out." "I'll be the judge
of that". No instinct to escape, crawling
over each other in an overly populated
tank, just lying there waiting to be fed
eating more than you need and wanting
more cause you never know if its
ever going to come again. Breeding
& eating & waiting & complaining &
praying,

~~The butter be being out slowly, did
he solidify into a pedophile.
sweat like butter melts and flow
through the valleys of ripe - old skin of
pink prunes~~

Starting from the arm pit of an old man,
~~and down~~
in a rush of slow motion - flood gates,
blown
wide - open, sweat ~~like~~ butter melts downward
through the valleys of ripe, pink-prune skin,
wrapped loosely around his ~~marble~~ arm,
Brittle
congregating at the tips of uncut,
Jaundiced fingernails, the beads meet and
Breed
~~and mix,~~ then jump to their death. ~~so~~
A splash
they land as ~~beads~~ ~~land~~ on smoothe thighs
mo - hair
of infants lying limp on beds of ~~angels hair~~
dirty books made him solidify into a pedophile.
Coalate Corelate
Corralate Coralate Solidiphile into A Pedfile
Corilate
I'm not well read, but when I do
read, I read well.
~~(scribbled out)~~
I dont have the time to translate
what I understand in the form of conversation.
had   most conversation
I exhausted ~~this~~ at age nine.
with   screams
I only feel grunts and tones and with
hand gestures and my body. ~~and tones~~ im deaf in spirit.

114

~~I keep myself~~

I purposely keep myself naive and away from
earthly information because its the only
way to avoid a jaded attitude.

everything i do is internally~~ed~~ subronciouse
because you cant rationalize spirituality
we dont deserve this privilege ⊕
~~I can only feel~~.

I cant ~~████~~ speak, I can only feel.
maybe someday Ill~~ ██~~ turn myself into
Hellen Keller by puncturing my ears
with a knife, then cutting my voice box
out.

If you want to know what I ~~██████~~
the after life feels like, then put on a parachute
go up in a plane, shoot a good amount of heroine
into your veins and immediately follow that with
a hit of nitrous oxide then jump.
or, set yourself on fire.

                                Youre

✓ IN Bloom
✓ Polly
✓ SAPPY
✓ Imodium
✓ PAY to play
✓ Somethings in the WAY
✓ Verse chorus verse
✓ Sliver
✓ P-Rock
✓ Lithium

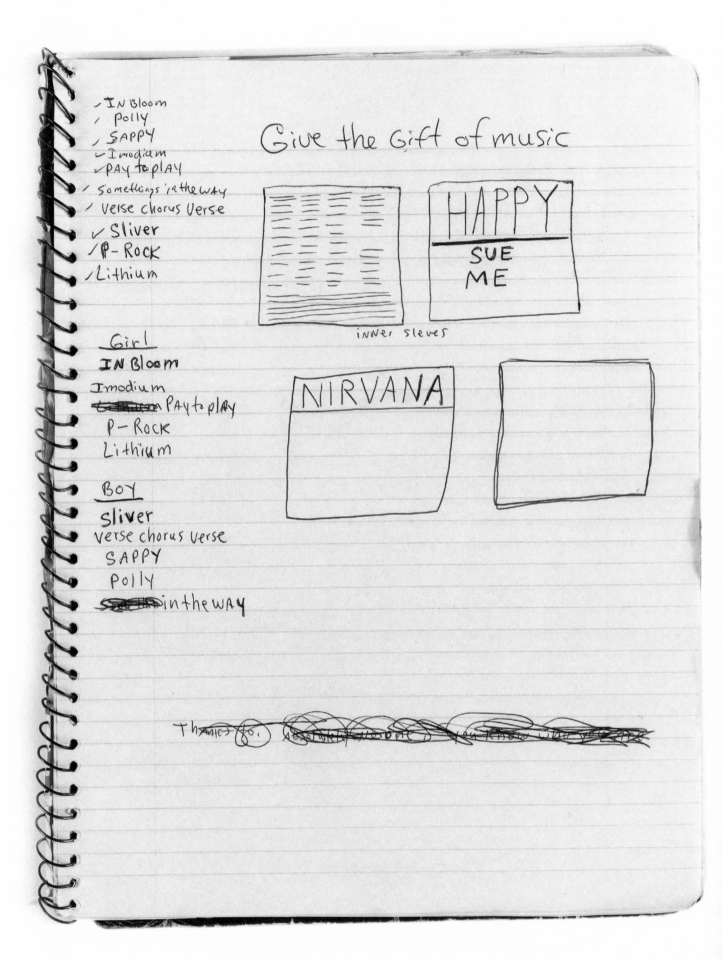

Give the Gift of music

HAPPY
—————
SUE
ME

inner sleves

NIRVANA

Girl
IN Bloom
Imodium
~~Lithium~~ PAY to play
P-Rock
Lithium

BOY
Sliver
Verse chorus verse
SAPPY
Polly
~~Somethings~~ in the WAY

Thanks to. ~~scribbled~~ you know who you are

116

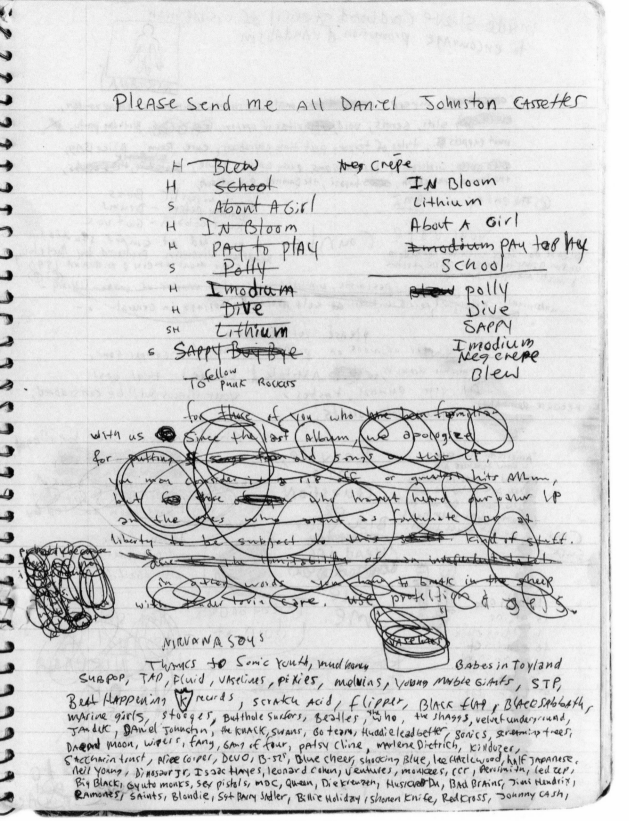

Please Send me All Daniel Johnston Cassettes

H — Blew   Neg Creep
H   School   IN Bloom
S   About A Girl   Lithium
H   IN Bloom   About A Girl
H   Pay to Play   ~~Imodium~~ Pay to Play
S   ~~Polly~~   School
H   Imodium   ~~Blew~~ Polly
H   Dive   Dive
SH   Lithium   Sappy
S   Sappy ~~Bye Bye~~   Imodium
         To fellow   Neg creep
            Punk Rockers   Blew

for those of you who have been forgotten with us since the last album, we apologize for putting old songs on this LP. You may consider it a rip off or greatest hits album, but for those of you who haven't heard our older LP and the ones who aren't as fortunate or at liberty to be subject to this kind of stuff. due to the limitability of an interfered to let in other words you have to break in the sheep with tender loving care. Use protection & gloves.

NIRVANA SOYS
Thanks to Sonic Youth, and early   Babes in Toyland
SUBPOP, TAD, Fluid, vaselines, pixies, melvins, Young Marble Giants, STP, Beat Happening K records, scratch Acid, flipper, Black flag, Black sabbath, Marine girls, Stooges, Butthole Surfers, Beatles, the Who, the shaggs, velvet underground, Tandik, Daniel Johnston, the Knack, swans, Go team, Huddie leadbetter, sonics, screaming trees, Daydream moon, wipers, Fang, Gang of four, patsy cline, marlene Dietrich, Kinduzer, Saccharin trust, Alice Cooper, Devo, B-52s, Blue cheer, shocking Blue, Lee Hazlewood, half Japanese, Neil Young, Dinosaur Jr, Isaac Hayes, leonard cohen, ventures, monkees, CCR, Aerosmith, led zep, Big Black, Gyuto monks, sex pistols, MDC, Queen, Die kreuzen, Husker Du, Bad Brains, Jimi Hendrix, Ramones, saints, Blondie, Sgt Barry Sadler, Billie Holiday, Shonen Knife, Redkross, Johnny cash,

inside sleeve cardboard stencil of visible man
to encourage promotion & vandalism

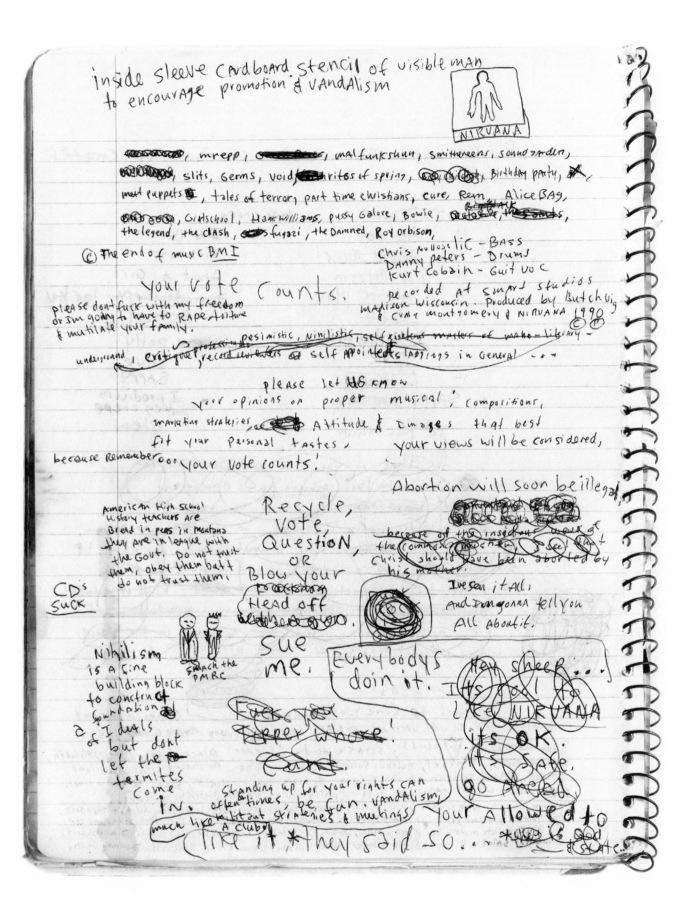

NIRVANA

~~xxxxxxx~~, mrepp, ~~xxxxxxx~~, malfunkshun, smithereens, soundgarden,
~~xxxxxxx~~, slits, Germs, void ~~xxxx~~ rites of spring, ~~xxxx~~, Birthday party, ~~x~~,
meat puppets, tales of terror, part time christians, cure, Rem, Alice Bag,
~~xxxxxxx~~, Girlschool, Hank williams, pussy galore, Bowie, ~~xxxxxxx~~, ~~xxxxxx~~,
the legend, the clash, ~~xxx~~ fugazi, the Damned, Roy orbison,

© The end of music BMI

chris novoselic - Bass
Danny peters - Drums
kurt Cobain - Guit voc

your vote counts.

please dont fuck with my freedom
or Im going to have to RAPE, torture
& mutilate your family.

recorded at smart studios
madison wisconsin. Produced by Butch vig
& craig montromery & NIRVANA 1990 ©

underground, critique protesting, pesimistic, Nihilistic, self existent master of maho - library -
record reviewers or self appointed scapings in General ...

please let us know
your opinions on proper musical, compositions,
marketing strategies, ~~xxxx~~ Attitude & Images that best
fit your personal tastes, your views will be considered,
because Remember... your vote counts!

Abortion will soon be illegal,
~~xxxxxxxxxxxxx~~
because of the insidious views of
the coming ~~xxxxx~~ see! that
christ should have been aborted by
his mother.

American High school
history teachers are
Bred in peas in montana
they are in league with
the Gout. Do not trust
them, obey them but
do not trust them.

Recycle,
Vote,
Question,
OR
Blow your
Head off

CD's
suck

Ive seen it All,
And Im gonna tell you
All about it.

Nihilism
is a fine
building block
to construct
a foundation
of Ideals
but dont
let the
termites
come
in.

sue
me.

Everybodys
doin it.

Hey sheep...
Its cool to
LIKE NIRVANA
its OK.
its safe.
go ahead

~~Fuck you perry whore!~~

standing up for your rights can
oftentimes, be fun, vandalism,
militant strategies & meetings
much like ~~a club~~
Your allowed to
like it, they said so...

smash the
PMRC

skate

119

I started it first
I started it first
I I was me
me
II I'm the one
I was the originator
I'll take the blame
me
it was me
I was the instigator
the grandfather
the first and foremost
I was doin it long
Before Anyone
It was me
I'll take all the blame
I'll take full responsibility
my fault
I started it all
I started it first
me
I'm the one
Blame me
point the finger at me
Heres my receipt
where do I sign?
give me whats owed to me
give me whats rightfully mine
give me what I deserve

I Deas for Video

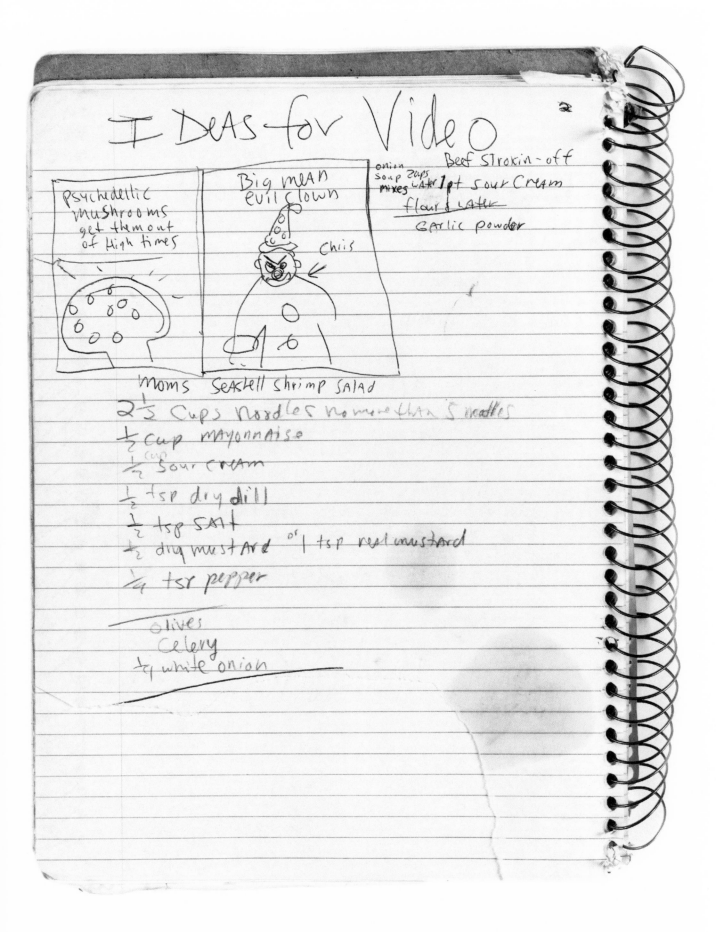

Beef Strokin-off

onion
soup zups
mixes water 1 pt sour cream
flour & water
garlic powder

Psychedellic
mushrooms
get them out
of High times

Big mean
evil clown

Chiis

moms   Seashell shrimp salad

2½ cups noodles no more than 5 noodles

½ cup mayonnaise

½ cup sour cream

½ tsp dry dill

½ tsp salt

½ dry mustard or 1 tsp real mustard

¼ tsp pepper

olives
celery
¼ white onion

K

1 ms 2 Henice 3 Bitch 4 Reynolds patti flae leis 5 6 7 Junior High
stinky   montesano   flxting stine
8 uncle Chuck & Joan summer monte grandpa cobain grandma 9 uncle Jim 10 mom 11 12 Gresay eshtr

It is time now for all the 'fortunate'
ones, the cheerleaders and the football
Jocks to strip down naked in front of
the entire school at an assembly and
plead with every ounce of their souls
for mercy and forgiveness, to
admit that they are wrong. They
are representatives of Gluttony and selfish
animalistic values and to say that they
are sorry for condoning these things
will not be enough, they must mean
it, they must have guns pointed to their
heads,   they must be petrified to ever
think of being the stuck up, self righteous,
segregating, guilt spreading, Ass Kissing, white,
right wing republicans of the future.

Kill the Rockefellers

IN Bloom
Lithium
Polly
☆ P Rock
Imodium

Pay to play
Sliver
Been A son
Sappy
☆ Verse Chorus Verse
☆ Something in the way

gotta find A WAY, A better wAy
to find A way

whatIneed
Someday
memoria
SPANK Thru
☆ Lounge Act
Second time
I dont have the Right
Dumb
Libido
~~P Rock~~ mommA

just because your paranoid
doesn't mean they're not after you

US out of ~~Americe~~ CANADA
~~US out of~~

God is Gay and so Am I

God is love love is blind and so Am I

I have no opinions
because I agree with everyone

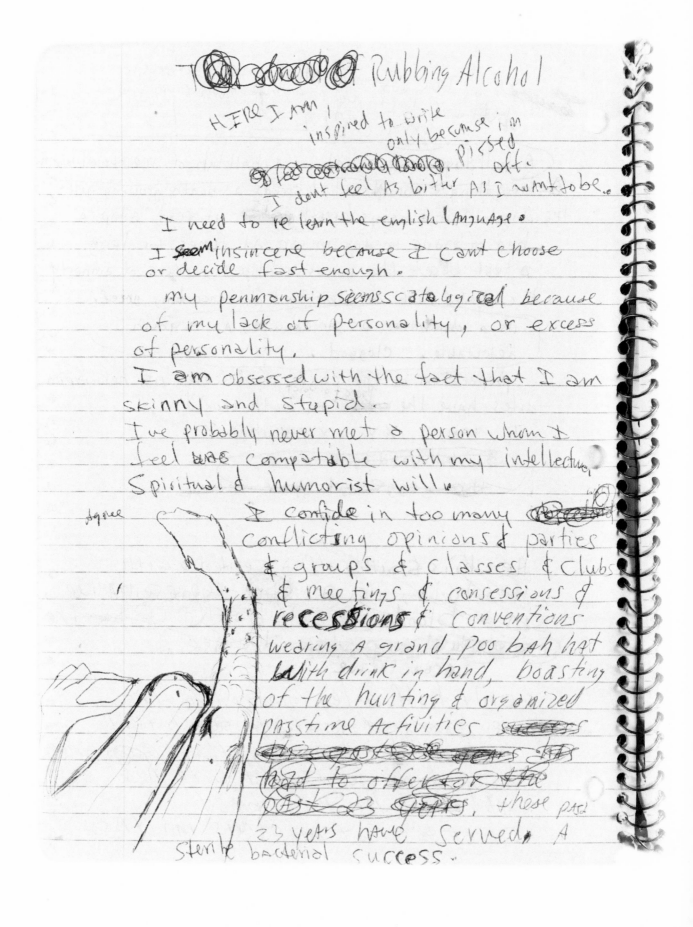

~~Tooooooooo~~ Rubbing Alcohol

HERE I AM,
      inspired to write
            only because im
                        pissed
                              off.
      ~~oooooooooooo~~ I dont feel as bitter as I want to be.

I need to re learn the english language.

I ~~seem~~ insincere because I cant choose
or decide fast enough.

   my penmanship ~~seems scatological~~ because
of my lack of personality, or excess
of personality.

I am obsessed with the fact that I am
skinny and stupid.

I ve probably never met a person whom I
feel ~~was~~ compatable with my intellectual,
Spiritual & humorist will.

agree   I confide in too many ~~oooooo~~
                  conflicting opinions & parties
                  & groups & classes & clubs
                  & meetings & consessions &
                  recessions & conventions
                  wearing a grand poo bah hat
                  with drink in hand, boasting
                  of the hunting & organized
                  passtime activities ~~xxxxx~~
                  ~~oooooooooooooooooooo~~
                  ~~had to offer for the~~
                  ~~past 23 years.~~ these past
                  23 years have served a
sterile bacterial success.

I've been to A lot of Bad poetry readings

Congratulations to cobession. sounds like perfume isn't extracted from disemboweled whale blubber anymore. chemicals are the thing of today, today ill take as many chemicals as i can get my greasy paws on, because this scent reminds me of you. just like they said it would in the commercial. yesterdays scent is still here today, I'm beached. flat out stranded and obsessed. Ive got to leave because your still here in my Air, fucking with my sense of smell, invading my air waves. your All over the sheets & in the bathroom, my couch reAks of you! youve left your underwear & coat & records & books & scent here,
IN MY place of recovery. the place where Ive craw off to die like A cat under A house After hes been hit, lying around writing

DAVE
(213) 654.   ) I dont invent subjects
                   of interest for conversation,
I dont have Anything to sAy or Ask, I
Just play Along. I'm A reActionAry
in A wAy, I just reAct to what others
sAy. I dont think & when I do I forget.
give me A leonard cohen Afterworld.

125

Opinion

Congratulations you have won — its a
years subscription of bad puns — and a
makce shift story of concern — and to
set it up before it burns — my
     opinion

Now there seems to be a problem here
the scale of emotions seem too clear —
Now they — Rise & fall like wall street stock
And they — Have an affect on our peace talks
     my opinion

MANDATORY Breeding laws
Sue ME
MANDATORY Abortion   VACCINATIONS Denied

~~Taking time to smear dignified street smart hipness into the carefully cultivated image they~~ ~~once presented~~, now faced with corporate trust, merging this happy day, This day giving amnesty to sacrilege. Only do I think when inspiration is so welcome ~~torme~~ from the allowance you give with the birth of ~~_____~~ Tongue. beyond Pissy complaints of ~~descriptive~~. Inspired, I sway back and forth between taking advantage of my position and giving up. Self appointed judges of review giving those with similar profit and potential the confidence to quit.

So your parents suck. ~~_____~~
Parents have always sucked. So your parents are really pretty cool? ~~_____~~ Other kids parents suck so fight for them. Revolution is no longer an embarrassment, ~~_____~~ thanks to inspiration. The politbureau questions sarcasm: maintain we must our ~~_____~~ ~~_____~~ righteously ~~_____~~ alternative opinions carved into our freshman year and slowly solidifying into the

JACKSON BROWN ~~Jimmy Buffet / Jame Taylor~~ kingdom by graduations end. At times its an excuse to delay the world we eventually take in the ass. Throw eggs at your enemy. A symbolic chicken foetus AT pro lifers.

I am a male, age 23 and I'm Lactating. my breasts have never been so sore not even after receiving Titty twisters from bully-school mates. They had hair down there long before I stopped playing with dolls. I haven't masturbated in months because I've lost my imagination. I close my eyes and I see my father, little girls, german shepherds & TU news commentators, but no voluptuous, pouty lipped, naked-females sex kittens, wincing in ecstasy from the illusory positions I've conjured up in my mind. No, when I close my eyes I see lizards & flipper babies, the ones who were born deformed because their mothers took bad birth control Pills, ~~in the sixties~~

I'm seriously afraid to touch myself.

Homage or Ripoff? I dont care, uh, I dont know.
Seems like finally the appreciation of things are
in order. there are a lot of things & bands to
be thankful for, yes, and everything sucks.
Too many compilations of present day bands paying
homage to old influential bands. Either
there are no good ones left to look forward to
or finally the undergrounds p-rock admittance,
to appreciation instead of Everything Sucks!
Clones of old, and the younger generation
never hardly heard old Aerosmith records or Rod Steward
& small faces so they have no sense of
pladgerism in the "now" bands paying homage
(supposedly) or keeping the faith.

Six strings, 24 notes
that repeat the same scale after 10, usually based
on 4:4 time signature, Rock and Roll: 30 years
= Exhausted! All the good old days!
The Now generation: unaware recession,
Technology finally caught up with us.
Hip hop/RAP? = for the time being, yes good
at least original, exhausted in 3 years.
women? yes. oppressed from chance
since beginning. probably some ideas left in
an unsaturated vagina.
Record store chains and RADIO play it
safe, target audience, what sells,
were completely at their mercy
it used to be the other way around.
Programmers & DJs: get into
Real estate!

I am in absolute and total support of: homosexuality, drug use, in experimentation (although I am living proof of harmful results from over indulgence) Anti oppression, ie: (religion, racism, sexism, censorship and patriotism) creativity through music, art, journalism, writing, Love, friendship, family, animals and full scale revolution violently protest organized, terrorist-fueled revolution.

You cannot de-program the Glutton.
You can only make them scared shitless to.
It would be nice to see the gluttons become so commonly violently attacked hunted down that they eventually they will either submit to the opposite of their ways or be scared shitless to ever leave their homes.

John lennon has been my Idol all of my life but he's dEAd wrong about revolution.
Sit on your ass and be beaten!
Bullshit!, Arm yourself, find a comp a representative of Gluttony or oppression and blow the motherfuckers head off. design manifestos with ideas, contacts, recruits, go public, risk jail or Assasination, or get employed by the target so its easier to infiltrate the system slowly sort the mechanics of the empire

Hi Eugene,

     Its eight o clock in the morning, that means its almost time for bed.

     Im on this rediculous sleeping schedule where I retire in the wee hours of morning and successfully avoid any hint of daylight. my skin is ~~death~~ 90th rock pale. I dont know if you have these things in Scottland but im considering joining a tanning bed salon, they are coffin/beds with haloid or flourescent light boulbs built into the sides and lid. ~~and~~ You lye down inside ~~to~~ fry away turning a crisp golden brown. we call ~~them~~ nuclear tans.

     lately my nipples have been really sore, can males lactate?   How have you been?

     As you probably know, we recorded mollys lips & son of a gun for a peel session and we were wondering if we could use the recordings for a promotional EP hopefully to be released in a few months. we dont expect to make a profit off of it because were keeping the price down, It's mainly a feature for our supposedly hip-alternative debut single "IN Bloom", the EP will have (if consented by us) IN Bloom, Sliver, D-7 by the wipers, Turn around by Devo, ~~and~~ mollys lips and maybe son of a gun. If we do make any money off of this then we'll surely devide it amongst the bands or we could talk about upfront advance for the use of the songs or whatever, it's legit!

were not on SubPop any more, our new label is DGC (Geffen).
we are label mates with Nelson!

I know this is starting to sound too business like
but I want you to have something for
giving us this ~~scribbled out~~
great honor ~~scribbled out~~
to play your songs, they mean a lot
to me. Without trying to be too embarrasingly
Sappy ~~scribbled out~~ I have to say the songs you
and frances have written are some of
the most beautiful songs ever and I just
feel like ~~everyone~~ should hear them.
Heres what the cover might look like ⟶

I had a really fine time
at the show we played ~~together~~
the video turned out good. you
want a copy? oh yeah, European
Video format, forget it.   geez I
Tape
dont know what else to say.
    please write me (if you want)
    and let me know how your
new band is coming along and
anything else thats on your mind.

            Love, your pal
            kurdt

NIRVANA Sings
the VASelines
wipers
Devo
&
NIRVANA

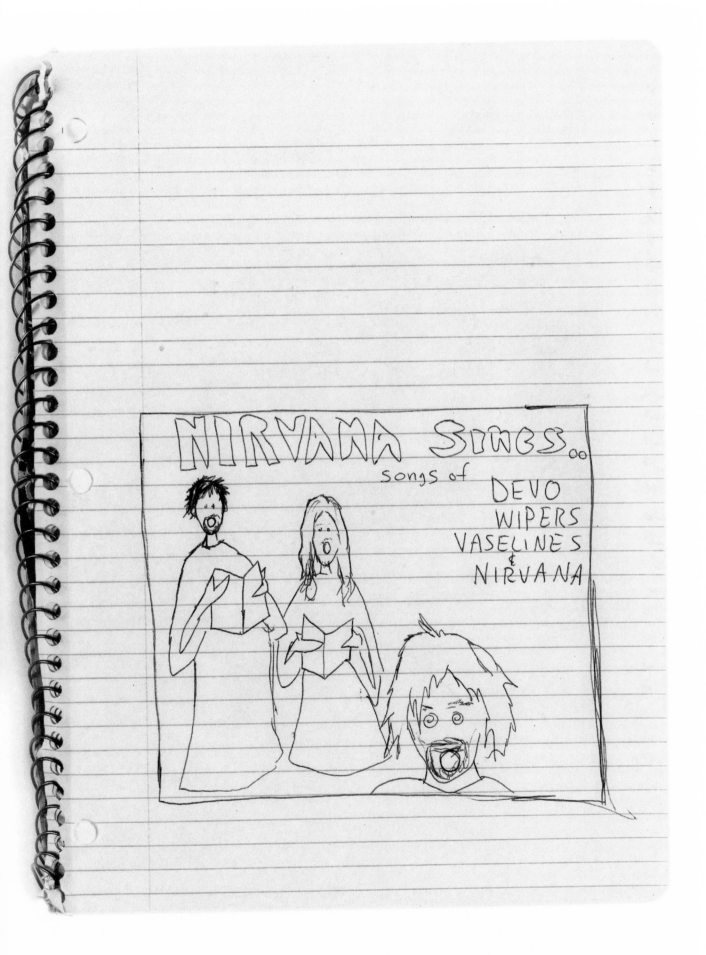

Bill price guns & roses   Chris thomas engineer   sex pistols

Gill Norton pixies

Allen moulder - my bloody valentine mixed Jesus & mary Chain

? & Barbiato - guns roses soundgarden

George Derkoulios - Black crowes   available last week of June

John Hanlon - Ragged glory freedom

Dave Jerden - Janes Addiction   Talking Heads Alice n Chains

Ed Stacium -   living Colour

Ron St Jermin - Anthrax Death Angel the Youth

scott Litt

And Hairy, sweaty, macho-sexist and racist Dickheads who
will soon drown in a pool of razor blades and sperm from
the uprising off your children, the armed and de-programmed
crusade, littering the floors of Wall Street with revolutionary debris,
assasinating both the lesser and greater of two evils, ~~getting~~   Botanical
~~absolute~~ bringing an everlasting sterile and bacterial, herbacious & corporate
cleansing for our ancestors to gaze in wonderment and awe.

will be
strung up
by their
Balls with
pages of the
scum manifesto
stapled to
their Bodys

The representatives of the American male **rapes**
in more ways than one.
~~oh well whatever, nevermind~~

posing as the enemy to infiltrate the mechanics of the empire
and slowly start its rot from the inside
    it's an inside job — it starts with the custodians And
the cheerleaders, oh well, whatever, nevermind.

mouth

sprinkler
camera lens

water supply

power

Food

Xerox

spray
paint

secret Handshakes

FIG. A

135

Cursed Aint the word

smells like Teen Spirit

It will be fun

Poppy plants are growing

Come out and play - make up the rules
have lots of fun we know we'll lose

Our little group has always been and
always will until the end

~~The~~ ~~other boycotters~~ don't deserve
to know oh no ~~I told a secret word~~
A Dirty word

Bend

pep Assemblys Become RALLYS

revolutionary debris litters the floor of Wall street, your children have taken over, you have been warned, the representatives of gluttony ~~and all the other~~ ~~neato things that~~ ~~that are related~~ will be given 24 hours to VACCUM and shave their ways or leave, or they will be weeded out ~~and~~ And assasinated with a HO to the back of the neck to SAVE Bullets

Club

load up on guns & bring your friends
I know I know ~~lets not pretend~~ it's wrong to
Take off your clothes I'll see you in court offend
~~to appear for~~ abort
~~to what you should~~ Abort
Abort

Special
we merge ahead this ~~happy~~ day
this day giving Amnesty to sacrilege

flyers fly

Learn All three chords ~~   ~~
~~down your competition is weak~~
~~get out of bed   asleep~~

store

Handle

A gift of choice I got from you

oh No I know A Dirty word

~~I'll take as much as you can I'll never know~~
~~when you'll run out~~

got from you

blemish
blush

Now I forget just why I taste - oh yeah
~~oh yeah~~ I guess It makes me smile
why dont you cry when I'm ~~far~~ AWAY
oh yeah we want whats best for you

what is
Hot

_ _ _ repeat   is something New

truth

The finest day Ive ever had

WAS when Tomorrow Never CAME
pull Away   I'm ~~~~ bad at what - I do best
            Im blessed to know   ~~Tame~~
And for this gift I feel blessed   that Most Are
                                        Tame
my credit rAn Away from me

with the light out It's less dangerous
Here we are now entertain us
I feel stupid And contagious
Here we Are now   Segregate us

A mulato   An Albino
A mosquito   my Libido
        YAY

come hang yourself with Umbilicle Noose

UH oh   oh No A Dirty word

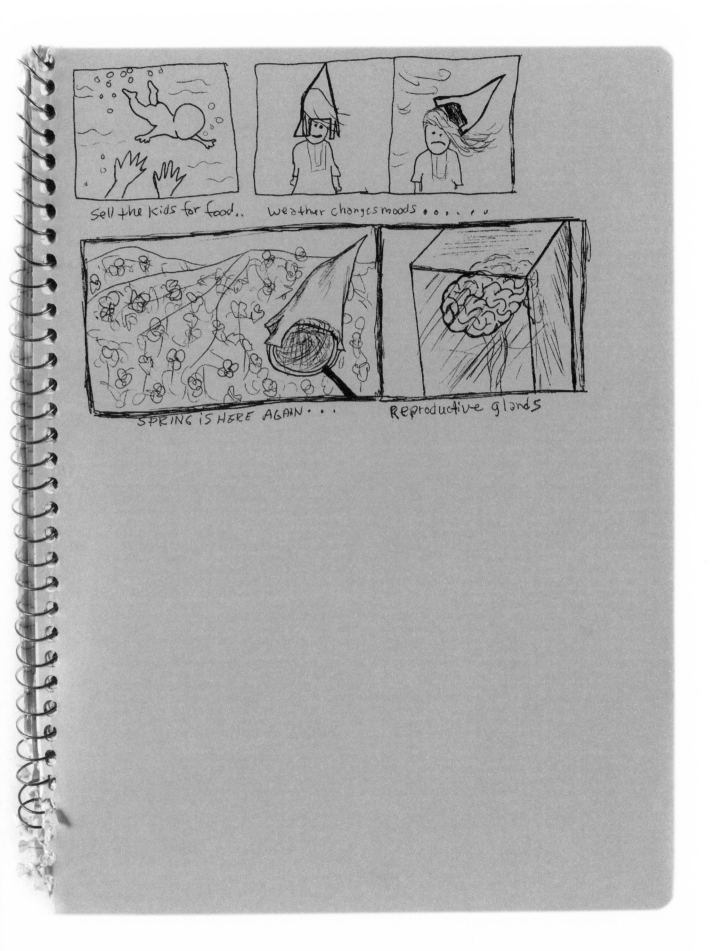

Lithium

① * Im so happy because today I found my friends
   Theyre in my Head.

 * Im so ugly but thats ok cause so Are you
   ~~And~~ ~~We~~ broke our mirror

② Sunday morning is ~~the da~~ every day for All I care
   And Im ~~not so scared~~ not scared
   Light my candles ~~in a daze~~ cause I found God
              Hey Hey Hey

   Im so lonely but thats ok I shaved your head
   And Im not sad

   And Just may be
   Im to blame for All I ve heard but Im not sure
        excited
   Im so ~~kissed~~ I cant wait to meet you
   there - but I dont care

   Im so horny thats ok my will is good
   ~~And I ve got food to tie me over band~~
   ~~Keep my mind on meeting you~~
   ~~And eat my friends Again And Again~~

   I ~~hate~~ you } Im not gonna crack
   I miss you }
   I love you
   I killed you

smells like teen spirit feel

Come out and play, make up the Ruler so stupid
I know I hope to buy the truth

Take off your clothes I'll see you in court
||||
hello
we know we'll lose but we wont be bored
Come out and play, make up the rules
It's not enough with golden tooths

Dyslexic idiot savant with bad hearing
load up on guns & bring your friends
The secret hand shakes pretend
were so stupid so lazy, blame our parents
talking freezes me
we're so lazy & so stupid
blame our parents
the stupids

Neurotically Lethargic

Tribe
Variety

So famous
entertaining your pamphlet
has been read
every night before bed
Undeserving

Our little group has always been, and always will
until the end
swore
We cut our hands & made a pact we're never going back

Tribe
territory
Leaving Passings
spraying
Your mark

A mulato an Albino
A mousquito my Libido

YAY

A deposit
for a bottle
stuck inside it
No Role model

A Denial

The same percent has always
been and always will until the end

say anything
just to have an
opinion

Who will be the King & Queen
of the Outcasted teens
I hate to use percentages It's nice to know there is
A choice

141

IN BLOOM

Sell the kids for food - weather
changes moods
    spring is here Again - re-Productive
glands

Hes the one who likes all the
pretty Songs - and he likes to sing
along - and he likes to shoot his
Gun   But He knows not
What it means knows not
what it means and I SAY AAHH

We can have some more
NAture is A whore
Bruises on the fruit
Tender Age in Bloom

I SAW Jesus's face in wood panelling   Tastes like chicken

Verse chorus Verse

Lucky Black sheep Blackmailed
I'll see you in court
I was so High that I scratched
until I Bled
At the end of Rainbows and
~~the end~~ of your Rope
I was drawn into the
mAgnet Tar pit ~~sucks~~ ~~Pool~~

Grass is greener over here
Leads to ~~~~ burning bridges clear
Reinventing what we knew
I can't wait until im sued   —

your the reason i feel pain
it feels so good to feel again

Saline on the ocean in A Tank of fumes
wheres my stamp collection? I'm becoming bored
Have another baby its not filled up yet
Ive Lost All my contacts and my lack of Iron
I SAW Jesus's image in wood panelling

correct change only
postage Paid

A three Hour tour

Buy my
Bottled
Sweat

He goes without saying

Spayed & neutered

lack of trouble

Verse Chorus Verse

Neither side is sacred - No one wants to
win - feeling so sedated think I'll just
give in - Taking medication till my
stomachs full - I'm A moody bABy

grass is greener - over here -
youre l

Reinventing what we knew
I cant wait until im sued

Drain you
Smells like   Power

Come as you are

Come as you are - as you were -
As I want you to be -
as a friend - as a friend - as an
old enemy - Take your time -
hurry up - the choice is yours -
dont be late - take a rest -
as a friend - as an old -
memoria memory ah

Come dowsed in mud - Soaked in Bleach
As I want you to be -
As a Trend as a friend as an old
enemy memoriah

B
4
3 64
8
4

You said that I remind you of yourself tomorrow

And I swear that I dont have a Gun

Lounge Act

You. — keepin everything in line
mastering the art to remind
begging me to lighten up
never seems to be enough
    Lounging in the sea
  and I've got this

I burnt my hands so I can't feel
I'll wet my bed to make you a deal
I'll gouge my eyes
 I'll wear High Heels
I'll wrack my brains to prove I can still
    smell Him on you

You— wishin everything away
Bring it back another day

Safety is a special suit
cover up a Home

ON A PLAIN

I'll start this off without any words
I got so High that I scratched till I bled

The finest day that I've ever had
was when I learned to cry on command

Chorus
I love myself Better than you I know its
wrong so what should I do

my mother died every night
It's safe to say don't quote me on that

The Black sheep got black mailed again
Forgot to put on the zip code

It is now time to make it unclear
to write off lines that don't make sense

Somewhere I have heard this before
In a dream my memory has stored
As defense I'm Neutered & spayed
What the Hell Am I trying to say?

one more special message to go
And then I'm done then I can go home

I'm on a plain I can't complain
I'm on a plane I can't complain

147

needed
Values
perspective
necessities
essentials

Mead

VERSE
CHORUS
VERSE
CHORUS
solo
Chorus
Chorus

120 sheets / college ruled
11x8½in/27.9x21.6cm

3 subject
notebook

06710   The Mead Corporation, Dayton, Ohio 45463

Hi, I'm 24 years old. I was born a white, lower middle class male off the coast of Washington state. My parents owned a compact stereo component system molded in simulated wood grain casing and a 4 record box set ~~of~~ featuring AM radios contemporary Hits of the early seventies called 'good vibrations' by Ronco. It had such hits as Tony orlando & Dawns "Tie a yellow ribbon" and Jim Croches "Time in a bottle". After years of my begging they finally bought me a tin drumset with paper heads out of the back of a Sears catalog. Within the first week my sister poked Holes in the heads with a screwdriver. I cried to "Seasons in the Sun".) My mother played a song by Chicago on our piano, I don't remember the name of the song but I'll never forget the melody. my Aunt gave me a blue Hawaiian slide guitar and Amp for my 7th birthday, she also during those first precious years had given me the first 3 beatles albums for which I am forever grateful knowing that my musical development would have probably ~~come~~ to a Hole ~~if~~ ~~~~ of tha If I had to soak up one more Year of the Carpenters and Olivia Newton John.

IN 1976 i found out that the beatles had been broken up since 71 ~~and I had never heard of~~ ~~Jimi Hendrix~~ My parents got a divorce so I moved in with my dad into a trailer park in an even smaller logging community.

My dads friends talked him into joining the Columbia record club and soon records showed up at my trailer almost once A week accumulating quite a ~~large records by 77~~ collection by 77

what dr? - witt
location? - lakewood community center
9112 ~~Header Sto~~ Lakewood dr Sw

Rooftop

Fig. A

Theres at least one form of social change that
the early 90's has brought, ~~~~~~~~~~~~
the attainment of finally accepting various styles
of music (and/or style of dress) ~~~~~~~~~~~~
~~Achieve~~ ♪ Amongst the youth.   This is the first generation
~~Accord~~ that has brought musical unity between them and their parents.
~~Unanimity~~ There TODAY is no generation gap. Since the
                                                god fearing
⟨AMOK⟩   white bread ratio
   PO Box 861867   Days of the late 40's
Terminal Annex   Just after the 2nd
Los Angeles, CA 90086-1867 world war.
                            Jitterbug
                Boogie, Skittle, hand jwin,
                woogie

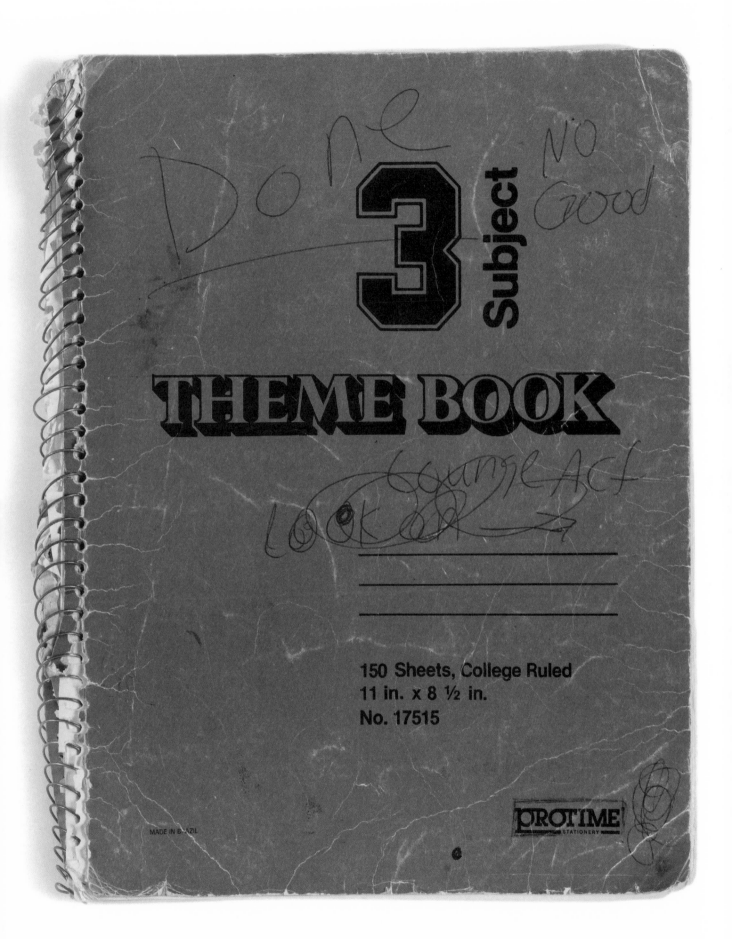

Se-ios	Smells like Teen Spirit
Gross HAPPY (X)	DRAin you
HAPPY	Lithium
HAPPY	In Bloom
SAD (F)	~~Come~~ AS You Are
SAD	Polly
MAD	Territorial Pissings
HAPPY Brees	(Immodium) (Verse Chorus Verse)
MAD	STAY AWAY
SAD	Something in the WAY
HAPPY (X)	ON A PLAin
HAPPY	Lounge Act

NIRVANA

Nevermind
~~Verse chorus Verse~~

Verse chorus Verse

★ SAPPY

Lounge ACT

ON A PLAin

Old Age

Thanks to : ~~Aron West~~, ~~Coldwarked~~, Jimmy Carter,
Susan Sylvers, ~~xxxxxxxxx~~, chad channing, Danny peters, the Melvins, Sonic Youth, mudhoney
Bob Goldthwait, the Vaselines, the wipers, the Beatles, the pixies, Black flag,
scratch Acid, ~~Hairy Joan Stein~~, Leadbelly, Night Flight, the stooges, ~~xxxxx~~ 70's ~~disco~~
~~xxxxxx~~, Olympia, Brothers Quay, flipper, Devo, Gang of four, aron Berkhart,
~~xxxxxxxxx~~, flipside, Beat Happening, H.R. Puffustuff, Mark Lanegan,
Tales of Terror, Butthole Surfers, New Nave theatre, REM, young Marble Giants,
Aerosmith, Led Zeppelin, Johnathan Poneman, Bruce Pavitt, TAd
~~Thanks to: Punk Rock~~
~~xxxxxxxxxxxxxxxxxxxxxxxxxxxxxx~~
~~You're probably respiring in one way or another~~

154

Thanks to: Un-encouraging parents everywhere for giving their children
the will to show them up, and to the white macho-american
Male for reminding the small percent who are capable of recognizing injustice
to fight you and learn from your sick, sadistic instinctual ways
May you rot in the very reason you even bother to stay alive whether

Thanks to ~~the representatives of~~ political figures and
those in the entertainment industry who are the
representatives of gluttony, for reminding us

Dont fuck your children
Dont beat your wife

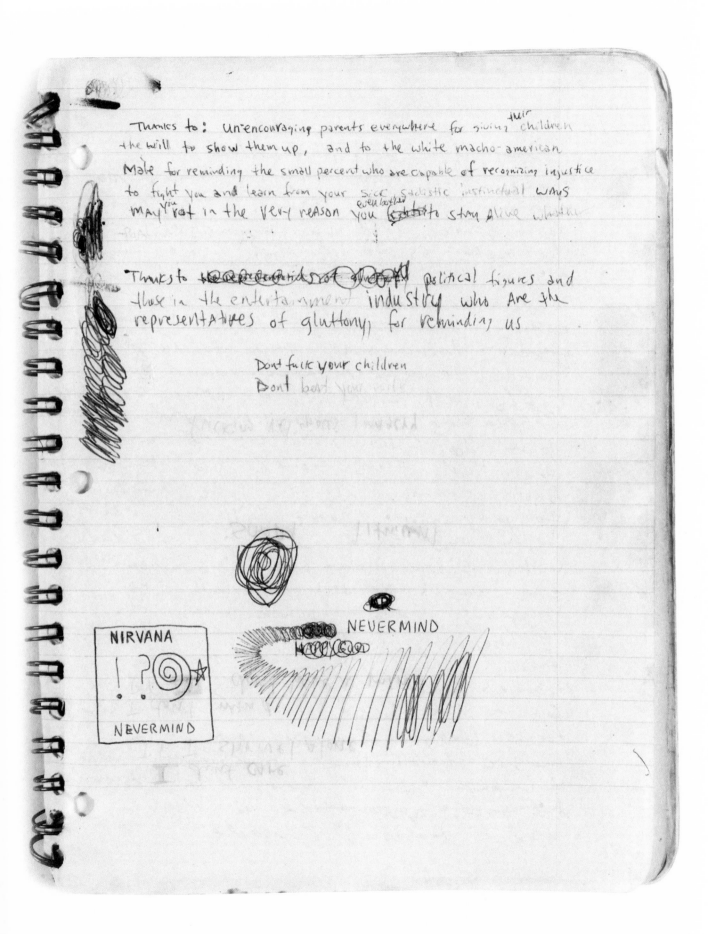

NIRVANA
! ? ⊙ ☆
NEVERMIND

NEVERMIND

155

"Rock is musical freedom. It's saying, doing and playing what you want. Nirvana means freedom from pain and suffering in the external world And thats ~~not~~ close to my definition of punk rock", exclaims guitarist Kurt Kobain. ~~the weight of that quote~~ Nirvana try to fuse punk energy with Hard rock riffs, all within a pop sensibility. "Speaking of sensibility" adds bass guitarist CHRIS NOVOSELIC "I wish we had more Sense, you know basic common sense, like rembering to pay your phone bill or rent". With the band inking a deal with D.G.C earlier this year the band is enjoying all the trappings that come with it. "Trapping schmapping fuck it man they throw us A few bones and the lights stay on for a while". rebuffs Drummer Dave Grohl. Cynical of the music industries machinery ~~The~~ Nirvana still Sees the nessessity ~~of such apparatice~~ to drive their musical Crusade.

<u>nevermind</u> the bands second album but 1<u>st</u> on a major label, culminated two years After the release of their first Album <u>BLEACH</u>. • "Kurt notes" ~~HAVE you~~ ever had ~~to find a job~~ a day when you were going to find a job then it was already two o'clock so you just blew it off? then the next day a friend comes over and hangs out, so you'll go tomorrow. Then well tomorrow, then tomorrow etc. etc. etc." However during this period the "Procrastination BUG" didn't AFFECT the bands Song writing. An E.P. was rel~~ieas~~ed <u>BLEW</u>. It had two songs off BLEACH (Love Buzz, BLEW) And two new songs (Been A Son, Stain). In the Fall of '90 the band rel~~ieas~~ed ~~the~~ single. SLiver/DIVE. ~~there~~ are also various studio Outakes making the rounds on the ~~greasy~~ sleazy Bootleg market.

only
live recordings

played
Nirvana ~~toured~~ alot also
during this period- three major
tours, including excursions to
England twice and elsewhere
in Europe once. they PLAyed
in Berlin one day after the
wall Fell. "~~People were crying~~
~~at the sight of bananas~~"
recalls Kobain. "there were
westerners offering people coming
over baskets of fruit and a
guy cried at the sight of
bananas". recalls Kobain.

the ~~bands~~ roots go back
to '87. It's the classic case
of two bored art students
dropping out and forming a ~~band~~.
Kobain, a saw black painter
specializing in wildlIFE And
SEA ScApe. Met Novoselic whose
passion was gluing sea shells And
driftwood on burlap potatoe
Sacks, at the acclaimed
Grays Harbon ~~school of north~~
institute of northwest crafts
Chris notes "when I saw Kobains
work I new there was something
special. I introduced myself
to him and asked what his
tryouts were on this ~~gift of desk~~

macaroni mobile piece I
was working on. He suggested
I glue glitter on it. from
then on it was an artistic
partnership that would spawn
the basis of what is the
magical collaboration of Nirvana
today" AFTER A long succesion
of/drummers Nirvana finally
~~XXXXXXX~~ ~~######~~

smells like Teen Spirit

needed
1. mercedes benz and a few old cars
2. Access to a Abandoned mall, main floor and one jewelry shop.
3. lots of fake jewelry
4. school Auditorium (Gym)
5. A cast of hundreds. 1 custodian, students.
6. 6 black cheerleader outfits with Anarchy A's (A) on chest

I had a cigarette in my hand, I thought it was a ~~cig~~ pen, I started writing a letter to my congressman, I told him about misery and corruption and bat cave ~~girls~~ – death rock girls who have danced at nude clubs in the city while trying to get off drugs and how they really, really care and if more vegetarian vampires could concentrate on ~~their~~ disclaimer-malpractice, sitting in the dark channelling the ~~a~~ combined energy of all the lost infant souls in this sphere or realm then we could all sip ~~their~~ licorice-flavored alcoholicbeverages down by the lazy rivers of ~~jordan~~ the rhone or ~~rhine~~. I dont have a beef with you, or a terrible, bitter, starvation for or in general. and its really hurting my lungs. this fag is marinated with the fear of the **KCPP** and laced with heavy metal-power ballads, giving me the clout to use stationary soaked in my favorite perfume and to put a stamp on upside down, only proves how much smell there is here and now, before ancestors and flint or even citrus colored sports bottles. well, get your priorities straight ~~you fucker. you mean nasty person~~.

His jaw dropped, and off slid his finely sculpted, bohemian goatee.

Breeders - pod   An epic that will never let you forget your ex girlfriend.

Pixies **surfer rosa** - A die-cast metal fossil from a space craft, with or without the fucking production.

Leadbellys last sessions (folkways) Vol. **1** - orgones, pyles, cells and he probably knew the difference between male and female hemp.

Vaselines - pink & Green EP's - Eugene + frances = documented love.

Young Marble Giants - Colossal youth - lying in an iron lung filled with luke warm water and epsom salts.

Wipers - "is this real? - yeah it **is**.

Shonen Knife - Burning farm EP - when i finally got to see them live, I was transformed into a hysteric nine year old girl at a Beatles concert.

Sex Pistols - Nevermind the Bollocks - one million times more important than the Clash

Jad fair - great expectations - with my headphones on, Jad and I ~~bootlegged~~ share "our little secret" walking thru shopping malls and airports.

YEAH, And then
they wiped their butts with it then
set it on fire!

rehabilitation, sympathy: Groups.
usually small, non profit or state funded
organizations directed to helping rape
victims cope with the crimes on them
brought upon them, also known as
rape crisis centers or planned parenthood
who by the way have now been just recently
been informed that it now is unlawful
soon will be unlawful for doctors at
workin, at these centers (usually on a
voluntary basis) to offer young pregnant
women every option available, meaning:
abortion They are not allowed to suggest
the option of abortion,
            I wonder if it was an intentional
    decision to leave out such for your part
    to leave out such a vital key words
such as "sympathy or rehabilitation", instead,
leaving the word 'group' all by its 'lonesome
to deceivingly make this rediculous little
quote to read as if I were attacking
other groups (meaning Rock Bands)
addressing rape and in turn
so righteously claiming, that the song polly
was intended to written as a rebuttle
towards these groups or (your so-called
(Rock bands) and to claim that this
our BAND (NIRVANA) have conciously decided that
it is a devout crusade for us, to, as A band,
to teach men not to rape. this is actually
we find it very frustrating to engage in a 2
Hour in depth interview and to waste these

this
is happening
in the U.S.
so why
should you
care.

it could
probably
happen
here
as
well.

not
print

for
inefficiently

two hours giving what we felt was a pretty insightful interview ~~and~~ then it turns out, only a ~~few~~ embarrasingly misquoted words were used, ~~making it~~ not to mention one quote literally stolen from another article a few months ~~later~~ ago, from NME (guns n roses attack) and in the end making it seem AS if were a band who have nothing better to say than garbled-second rate political rantings, we are not politically correct, but yes we do ~~feel~~ have opinions on these ~~matters~~ but we don't deserve the illusive display ~~of the next guns and roses~~ ~~your most responsible for the exxaggerated~~ commercial Hype

Being solely A political band, it's quite obvious ~~that~~ were not qualified or prolific enough to ~~even~~ try. thats why 90% of our interviews consist of half witted talk about music or our pets and when squeezed out of us about 10% of sincere, politically personal viewpoints revealed, and why is this? learning the hard way, ~~to~~ not ~~be~~ able to trust the majority of the incestually-competetive english journalist. talk about politics shall we? how many ~~sadistic~~ times have journalists of both papers one another

stabbed in the back, lied or provided favors
in order to beat one another for a cover story
~~with~~ with the same band? er, just a guess.
sensationalist tabloids are quite harmless and
it's understandable why they are needed when
the majority of present rock bands have
nothing to say musically but musical inspiration seems
to have been deformed by the vicious and
self serving pleasure of the journalist which
naturally incites bands to become paranoid
Defensive, Jaded, abusive and uncooperative.
the english journalist is a ~~masochistic~~
second rate self apointed judge who couldnt
make it to becoming a ~~therapist~~ mental therapist,
theyre enemic, clammy, physically deformed,
gnome-like, internally upset with a dysfunctional
ability to stabilize a relationship (except
with eachother) and sincerly masochistic
who would bathe in the glamour of
nude photos of themselves with handcuffs
behind the back, on their knees wearing
a diaper with a ~~scrawlotare~~ rubber
cock stuffed in their mouths, and these
photos pasted on every cover magazine
in Europe.   the rivals and the poachers
shall one day ban together ~~to~~ print
one tabloid ~~to~~ monthly.

and the weak crumbs will report to
the custodial arts. ~~schools~~

we
gleefully
decline
the
opportunity
to
Be
raped
by
the limey
Journalist.
By saying to
future interview?
No thanks
No thank
you

love kur-d-t Koebane

Hi,

Yeah, all Isms feed off one another, but at the top of the food chain is still the white, corporate, macho, strong ox ~~of~~ male. Not ~~redeemable~~ as far as im concerned. I mean, classism is determined by sexism because the male decides whether

All other isms ~~still~~ exists ~~still~~. its up to men. ~~RACISM~~ ~~SEXISM~~ ~~except~~

Im just saying that people cant deny any ism or think that some are more or less subordinate. ~~But its still think that in order to~~

except for sexism. He's in Charge He decides. I still think that in order to expand on all other isms, sexism has to be blown wide open, ~~its almost when you~~

Its almost impossible to de program the incestually-established, male oppressor, ~~but the~~ especially the ones whove been weaned on it thru their familys generations, like die hard N.R.A freaks and inherited, corporate, power mongrels, the ones whove were born into no choice but to keep the torch and only let sparks fall for the rest of us to gather at their feet. But there are thousands of Green minds, young gullable 15 year old Boys out there just starting to fall into the grain of what theyve been told of what a man is supposed to be, and there are plenty of tools to use, ~~the most~~ the most effective tool is entertainment. The entertainment industry is just now

starting to accept (us) (mainly because of trendy
falseness in environmentally, socially concience
hypeie; the new 90's attitude, which is
at a total standstill because of the
patriotic, aftermath of the war and all its
Nuremberg rally-parades) but they're using
mediA! Media. Major labels. (
~~The~~ evil corporate Oppressors, (god I need
a new word!) the ones who are in kAhoots
with the government, the ones the underground
movement went into retaliation against in the
early 80's) The corporations are finally allowing ~~subversive~~
supposedly subversive, alternative thinking
bands to have a loan of money to expose
their crusade, ~~with these~~ obviously they
arent ~~doing this~~ forking out loans for this
reason, but more because it looks to be
a money making, comodity, but we can
use them? We can pose as the
enemy to ~~to~~ infiltrate the mechanics of
the system to start its rot from the
inside. Sabotage the empire by pretending to
play their game, compromise just enough to
call their bluff. And the hairy, sweaty,
mAcho, sexist dickheads will soon drown in
a pool of razorblades and semen, stemmed
from the uprising of their children, the armed
and deprogrammed crusade, littering the floors
of Wall street with revolutionary debris.
Assasinating both the lesser and greater of two
evils. bringing an everlasting, sterile and bacterial
herbacious and botanical corporate cleansing for our

ancestors to gaze in wonderment and Awe. AWE!
geezus christ. (repeat): posing as the enemy
to infiltrate the mechanics of the empire and
slowly start its rot from the inside, it's an
inside job - it starts within the custodians
and the cheerleaders. And ends with the entertainers.
~~they~~ The youth are waiting, impatiently.
Homophobe VACCECTOMY.
    Its like what Kathleen said about how in school
there was this class that you went to and they
were teaching the girls how to prepare themselves
for rape and when you looked outside and saw
the rapers out outside playing football and
you said "They are the ones who should be in
here being taught not to rape".
    How true. Suck em in with quality
entertainment and hit em with reality.
    The revolution will be televised.
        Theres this new 24 hour channel on cable called
the 90's, which is available only in a few states so far
and it's magazine version can be seen on PBS
(public broadcasting system) ~~at least~~ once a week.
    It's pretty damn informative and it exposes
injustices ~~and stuff~~ in a kind of conservative -
/liberal format, but its new so it has to be that
way. Ive seen it a few times and really liked
it. Also Night flight is back. You know,
the show that used to play new wave theatre?
        we plan to use these shows and ~~others~~ other
if given the chance.   Yeah I know, I'm a ~~con~~
Confused, uneducated, walking cliche, but I dont need
to be inspired any longer, just supported.

Oh yeah, Gluttony, I almost forgot Gluttony. The band now has an image: the anti-gluttony, materialism & consumerism image which we plan to incorperate into all of our videos. The first one "Smells like teen spirit" will have us walking through a mall throwing thousands of dollars into the air as mall-goers scramble like vulchers to collect as much as they can get their hands on, then we walk into a jewelry store & smash it up in anti-materialist fueled punk rock violence. then we go to A pep Assembly at a High school And the cheerleaders have Anarchy As on their sweaters and the Custodian-militant-revolutionarys hand out guns with flowers in the barrels to all the cheering students who file down to the center court and throw their money & jewelry & Andrew dice Clay Tapes into A big pile then we set it on fire and run out of the building screaming. Oh, didnt twisted sister already do this?

Things that have been taken from me within the past 2 months: I wallet, drivers license etc.. $2100 three guitars (including the moserite) all my neato 70's effect boxes, apartment and phone. but I got a really neato left handed fender Jaguar, which is in my opinon, almost as cool as a mustang. So I consider it a fair trade for the moserite.

while staying in LA.
We almost got killed by gang members.
well, sort of.

Dave Franz and I were in the parking lot
of a famous, female-mudwrestler-night club
scoring lewds, when all of a sudden two
gass guzzling cars pulled up next to us and
five cho-los with knives and guns walked
over to the car closest to ours and started yelling
& cursing in gang lingo at eachother. But then
by the motto of "To protect and serve" the
cops show up, which insighted the gang
bangers to flee away in their cars, resulting
in a hot pursuit - Car Chase. There were
even hellicopters with search lights.

Needless to say we scored our lewds and
split.   We played a really fun show with
fitz of Depression at a really small coffee house
called the jabberjaw.   We were indescribably
fucked up on booze and drugs,   out of tune
and rather uh, sloppy. It took me
about fifteen minutes to change my guitar
string while people @ heckled and called
me drunk Robyn Zander. (cheap trick lead singer?)

After the show I ran outside and vomited.
then I came back in to find Iggy pop there
so I gave him a sloppy - puke breath kiss
and hug. He's a really friendly and cool
and nice and interesting person. It was probably
the most flattering moment of my life,

As you may have guessed by now Ive
been taking a lot of drugs lately
  It might be time for the Betty Ford Clinic
or the Richard Nixon library to save me
from abusing my enemic, rodent-like body
any longer. I cant wait to be back
at home (wherever that is) in bed, neurotic
and malnourished and complaining how the "weather
sucks" and its the whole reason for my
misery. I miss you, Bikini Kill.
  I totally love you.
              Kurdt

There is a small percent of the population
who were **BORN** with the ability to
detect injustice. they have Tendencies
to question injustice and to look for
answers (by their oppressors standards. in ways that would
be considered abnormal. They have Tendencies
and talents in the sense that they know from
an early age that they have the gift to
challenge what is expected of their future.

These kids are usually hyperactive, uncontrollable
brats who never know when to quit because their
so wrapped up in whatever their trying to prove,
that they eventually offend someone, not meaning
to of course. This is good.

They usually go through childhood thinking
their special. its partly instinctual and maybe
they've been told by their parents or teachers,
maybe theyre put in a gifted childrens —
over achiever class in grade school. for whatever
reason they end up molding into a person
aware of their abilities and not understanding
them and having bloated egos caused by
societys insistance that those with an
overly-functional insight should be praised
and considered to be on a higher level of
easy access toward success. Eventually
they beome totally confused and bitter
adolescents who tend to see nothing but injustice
because by that time they (usually) have
had the chance to be exposed to others
like them who learn from their gifted, bohemian
ancestors.

that their special.

Ancestors

The larger percent who have and always will dominate the smaller percent _{simply because they outnumber} we're not **BORN** with even the slightest ability to comprehend injustice. There are the stump dump _{Average Joe} Garbagemen ^{or Lawyers} of life.

Its not their fault because ~~they~~ physically **lack** that special, extra group of cells in the brain ~~that~~ welcome a questioning conciousness.

This is definitely Not hereditary.

It is definitely not their fault.

~~They~~ aren't simply misguided.

Of course the extremes ~~of~~ and levels of the ability to detect injustice range ~~to~~ all levels.

<u>not described</u> these people usually fit in the bracket that
<u>AS</u> could be ~~easily~~ compared ~~to~~ the level of one who is marginally retarded.

You know, the ones who have the symptoms of mongoloid rings around the eyes yet ~~they can still~~ act on prime time television dramas.

All other so called talents like, dance, singing, acting, wood carving and Art is mostly a developmental culmination of exercise ~~trying to attain~~ perfection thru practice

No True talent is ~~ever~~ fully organic.

<u>born</u> Yet the obviously superior talented have
<u>passion</u> not only control of study but that extra special, little gift ~~got~~ at birth — fueled by passion.   A built in, totally spiritual, unexplainable, New Age, fuckin, cosmic energy bursting love for passion.

And yes, they are an even smaller percent amongst the small percent. And they Are special! mistrust All Systematizers.

All things Cannot be evaluated to the point of total Logic or science. No one is special enough to ~~realize~~ Answer that.

This is not to be taken seriously,
This is not to be read as opinions.
It is to be read as poetry.
Its obvious that I am on the
educated level of about 10th grade in
High school. Its obvious that these
words were not thought out or even
re-read, ~~discarded as~~ this writing
style is what I like to call thru the perspective
of a 10th grader, her/his attempt at showing that no
matter what level of intellizence one
is on, we all question love and lack
of love and fear of love.

Its good to question authority and to fight it
just to make things a bit less boring,
but ive always reverted back to the the
conclusion that man is not redeemable
and words that dont necesarily have their
expected meanings can be used descriptively
in a sentence as Art. True english is so
fucking boring. And this little pit-stop
we call life, that we so seriously worry
about is nothing but a small, over the
week end jail sentence, compared to what
will come with death.
life isn't nearly as sacred as
the appreciation of passion.

its good
to question
Authority
but we never
came to the
same conclusion
that man is
not redeemable
And this
little pit-stop
we call life
that we so
seriously
worry
about is
nothing
but A few
Sentences
Compared
to
what will
come with
Death.

175

If were going to be ghettoised, I'd rather be
in the same slum as bands that are good
like mudhoney, Sears yzard, the Melvins and Beat happening
rather than being a tennant of the Corporate Landlords
regime.
I mean, were playing the Corporate game and
were playing as best as we can suddenly we
found ourselves having to actually play instead of using the
Corporations great distribution while staying in our little world
because we sold 10 times more the amount of records
we had expected to sell. It's just a shock
to be doing interviews with magazines that I
don't read

positive>

there are a lot of bands who claim to be alternative
and they're nothing but stripped down, ex sunset strip
hair farming bands of a few years ago
I would love to be erased from our association with
pearl Jam or the Nymphs and other first time offenders.

Alternative bands have tried to   the general public
every year since the sex pistols and have failed every time
not the fault of the bands but the times weren't right,
the Reagan years were so effective in keeping out
Any chance of a better concience which is why
there were so many great indie · do it yourself bands throughout
the 80's as suberts towards Reagan because he was such a
creep.

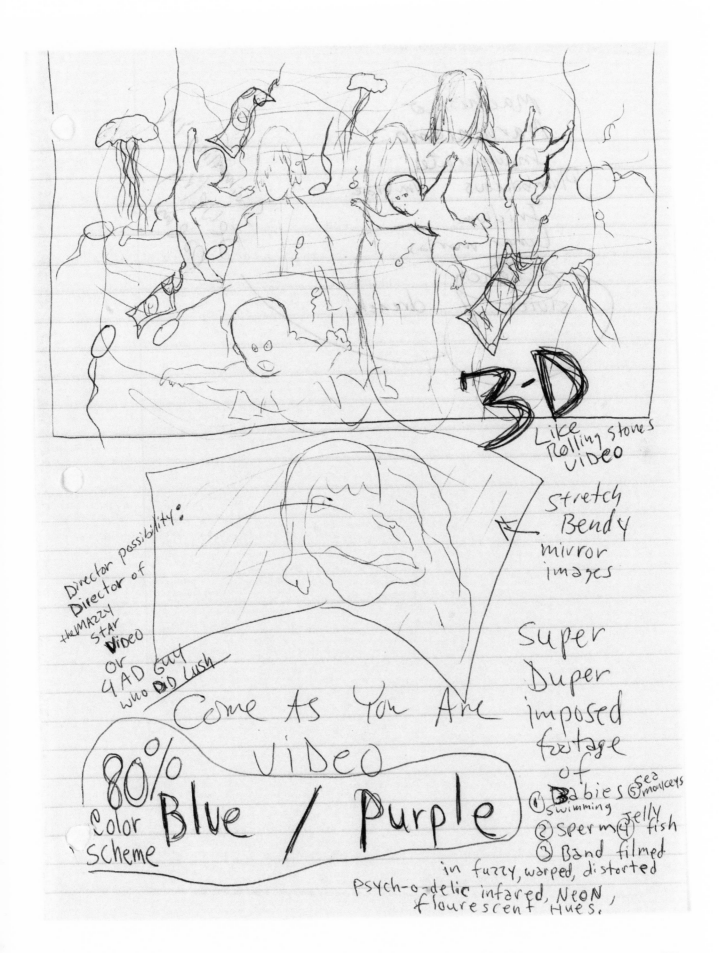

3-D

Like Rolling stones video

Director possibility:
Director of the MAZZY STAR video
or 4AD guy who DID LUSH

Stretch Bendy mirror images

Super Duper imposed footage of
① Babies swimming ⑤ Sea monkeys
② Sperm ④ Jelly fish
③ Band filmed

in fuzzy, warped, distorted psych-o-delic infared, NeoN, flourescent Hues.

Come As You Are Video

80% Color Scheme Blue / Purple

MElViNS

They have Reagan or Bush vote Republican
stickers on the bumper of their Van
to fend off nasty Rodney King Cops

All three members consistently sculpt various models displays
of the Goatee facial hair fashion   oh except for peach fuzz,-
pie eyed, baby face, Sometimes pinch an inchish, sometimes Annorexorcist,
skin tight purple Levis, Jimmy from HR Puffnstuff wearin haircut,
ex -Tea head, Smoking non-smoker   Dale All around nice Guy Dale Crover

Its hard to decipher the difference between
a~~n~~ sincere entertainer and an honest swindler.

I've ~~sorted~~ violently vomited to the point of
my stomach literally turning itself inside out to show
you the fine hairlike nerves I've kept and raised
as my children, garnishing and marinating Each one
as if God had fucked me and planted ~~these~~ precious
little eggs. and I parade them around in peacock
victory~~us~~ And maternal pride like a whore relieved
                                                    promoted
from ~~the~~ duties of repeated rape and torture,^ to a
more dignified ~~promotion~~ Job of just plain old every day,
good old, wholesome prostitution. My feathers are my pussy.
                CARtoon
                                    offering
        oh how I love the brutal effect of just one
        word ~~offered~~ to ponder like....
                Cartoon
        fuck man, think about it,
                CARtoon
                HEAVY man
                HEAVY

I f you think everythings been said and done
        then how come nothing has been solved
                and resolved?
                I Ask you.
        Sarcastically with a sneer. in A 90's way.
                kinda uh, defensively to say the least and to do
                                                         the worst.

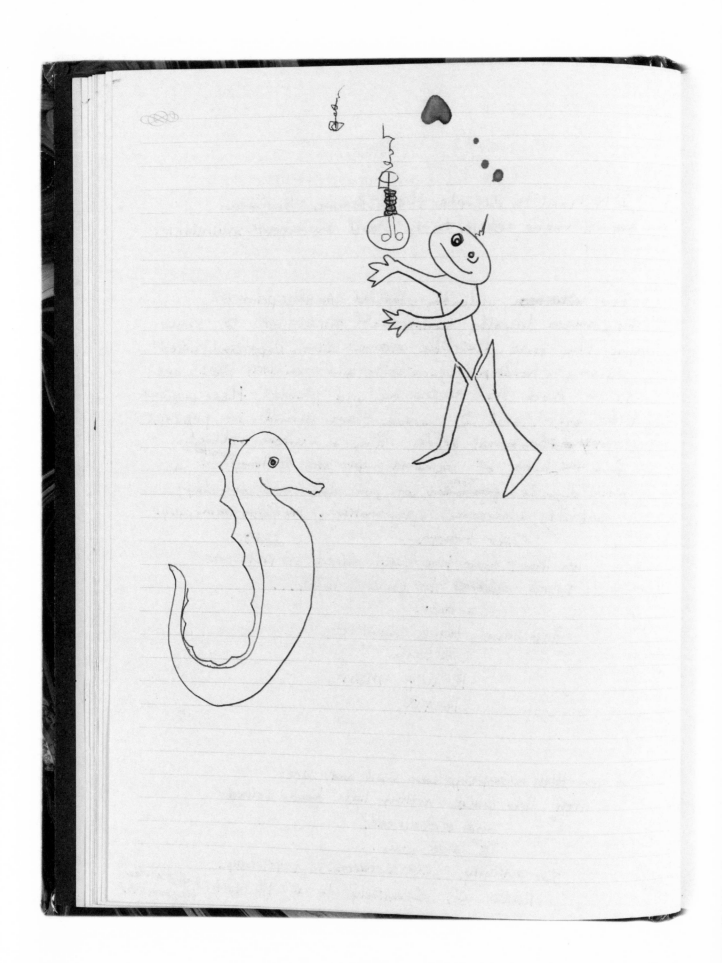

kind of
I feel like a dork writing ~~a de~~ about
myself like this as if I were an
American pop-Rock ~~Icon~~ demi God, or
"A self confessed product of corporate-packaged
-rebellion, but Ive heard so many insanely
exhaggerated stories or reports from my
friends and Ive read so many pathetic
second rate, freudian evaluations from interviews from my childhood
up until the present state   ~~I just cant handle the success!~~
of my → personality and how Im A notoriously
~~fucked up~~ Heroine addict, Alcoholic,
selfdestructive, yet overtly sensitive
frail, fragile, soft spoken, narcoleptic,
~~Rock~~ Neurotic, little piss ant who At any
minute is going to O.D. Jump off a roof
wig out ~~crazy~~. Blow my head off or All 3 At once.
Oh Geez GAWD I cant handle the success!
Guilt the success! And I feel so incredibly
Guilty! for Abandoning my true commrades
                      the ones who Are devoted.   the ones
who were into us A few years Ago
                My In 10 years
And ~~After~~ ~~when~~ ~~is~~ As memorable As KASA 700 500
when NIRVANA becomes   that same,
~~in 10 years~~ ~~the same~~ very small percent
will come to see us at reunion gigs
sponsored by Depends diapers, bald fAt,
                                           Amusement
still trying to RAWK. At ~~waterslide~~ PARKS .
SAturdays
~~No~~ Puppet show, Rollercoaster & NIRVANA

Ask Jenny Tumi if we can re-print her how to record a record essay, for this fanzine.

~~Since~~ After all the hype and oogling over us this past year I've come to two conclusions,

1: we've made a way better commercial record than Poison,

2: There are quadruple the amount of Bad Rock Journalists than there are bad Rock Bands.

Well for those of you who are concerned with my present physical and mental state.

→ I Am Not A Junkie.

I AM NOT GAY Although I wish I were, just to piss off Homophobes

I've had a rather unconclusive and uncomfortable stomach condition which ^{for the past 3 years} by the way is not related to stress which ^{also} means it is not an ulcer, because there is no pattern to the burning, nauseous pain in my upper abdominal cavity, I never know when it will ~~come on~~ happen, I can be at home in the most relaxed atmosphere sipping ~~Boric Acid~~, ~~and~~ ☞ natural spring water, No stress, No fuss and then Wham! like a shot gun: Stomach Time, then I can play 100 ~~shows~~ live performances in a row Guzzle Boric Acid & do ☞ a zillion television interviews and not even a burp. This has left doctors with no ideas except ^{the usual:} here Kurt try another Peptic ulcer pill and lets jam this fibre optic

~~As~~ perplexed

this has left many doctors perplexed

182

tube with a (video) camera in it down your throat (its)

[Called an Endoscope]

for the 3rd time and see whats going on in there Again. Yep your in pain alright try eating ice cream from now on. Your stomach is extremely inflamed and reciting

Please lord ~~let me have a disease~~ fuck hit records just let me have my very own unexplainable rare stomach disease Named After me.

And the title of our next double Album. "Cobains disease". ~~the endoscope is great for~~

~~A video and there just about finished with the~~

A rock opera which is all about vomiting, gastric juices being a borderline Annorexic ~~xxxxx~~ Auzhwitz - Grunge - Boy. And with it an accomanying endoscope Home- video. ~~xxx~~ So After protein drinks and doctor after doctor I decided to relieve my pain with Heroine small doses of for a walloping 3 whole weeks, but then I served as a band-aid for a while the pain came back so I quit. It was a stupid thing to do And I'll never do it again and I feel real sorry for Anyone who thinks they can use heroine as a medicine because um, duh it dont work. drug withdrowal is everything youve ever heard, you puke, you falail around, you sweat, you shit your bed just like that movie Christiane F. ~~I dont feel sorry for anyone~~ ~~xxx uses your~~ It's evil, leave it alone

becoming a vegetarian, exercise, stopping smoking

I'm not stressed   I am the product of 7 months of
I just sit back   screaming at the top of my lungs almost every night
and laugh
                    7 months of jumping around like a retarded wheelchair monkey
The cherub little scruff 7 months of answering the same questions over and over
you've grown to know from the picture on the back of Nevermind is
proof that film adds 10 pounds to your body, because I've been the same bird weight
ever since my last excuse which is...
I'm really bored with everyones concerned advice
like: "man you have a really good thing going
your band is great, you write great songs, but
hey man you should get your ~~shit together~~
personal shit together. Dont freak out
and get healthy. Gee I wish it was as
easy as that but, honestly I didn't want
all this attention but I'm not freaked out
li~~ke~~ ~~everyone would like to believe~~ which is something a lot of people would like to see . Its
an entertaining thought to ~~own your body~~
~~own~~ watch a (public domain) A Rock figure whos
mentally self destruct, but I'm sorry
friends I'll have to decline. Maybe
Crispin Glover should ~~start~~ join our band.
     And at the ~~day~~ end of the day, instead of plotting how
I can escape this ~~life~~ I just simply
have to laugh. I find it really funny. It feels as if weve
almost, pulled a minor Rock-n-Roll swindle
because I'm not nearly as concerned
with or about myself or anyone
as the media would have us believe
   I think the problem with our story is that
   there isn't an exciting enough truth for A Good story.
Well I've spewed enough, probably too much
   but oh well, for every one ~~self appointed~~ opinionated,
      pissy, self appointed Rock-judge curmudgeon theres A thousand
                                                       Kids.

OH THE GUILT   THE GUILT   (by: KurDt disclaimer-boy)

I kind of feel like a dork writing about the band and myself like
this as if i were an American pop-rock icon, demi god or a self confessed
product of pre packaged, corporate rebellion. But ive heard so many insanely
exhaggerated wise tales and reports from my friends, and ive read so many
pathetic, second rate,freudian evaluations from interviews, regarding
our personalities and especially how im a notoriously fucked up heroine
addict, alcoholic, self destructive, yet overly sensitive,frail,meek,
fragile ,compassionate, soft spoken,narcoleptic, NEUROTIC,little,piss ant
who at any time is going to O.D , jump off a roof and wig out, blow my
head off or all three at once because I CANT HANDLE THE SUCCESS! OH THE
SUCCESS! THE GUILT! THE GUILT! OH, I FEEL SO INCREDIBLY GUILTY! GUILTY
for abandoning our true comrades. the ones who are devoted. the ones
who have been into us since the beginning. the ones who (in ten years
when were as memorable as KAGA GOO GOO) will still come to see NIRVANA
at reunion gigs at amusement parks. sponsored by depends diapers, bald
fat and still trying to rawk.   MY favorite reoccurring piece of advice
from concerned idiots is:"Man, you have a really good thing going.
your band is great.you write pretty good songs and youve sold a shit load
of records but,hey man, you should get your personal shit together. dont
freak out and get healthy." Gee I wish it was that easy but honestly, I
didnt want all this attention, but im not FREAKED OUT!which is something
a lot of people might like to see. Its entertaining to watch A rock figure
whos become public domain mentally self destruct. But im sorry ill have
to decline. Id like to freak out for you . maybe Crispin Glover should
join our band. At the end of the day I laugh my ass offk knowing ive gotten
about 30¢ from this dork. Sometimes it feels as if weve pulled a minor
rock and roll swindle because im not nearly as concerned with or about
myself, the band or anyone as much as the media would like us to believe.
I think the problem with our story is that there isnt an exciting enough
truth for a good story. Oh, and another thing. I am not a heroine addict!
for the past three years ive suffered a rather unconclusive and uncom
fortable stomach condition. which by the way is not related to stress
which also means is not an ulcer because there is no pattern to the burn
ing , nausious pain in my upper abdominal cavity. its like russian roulette,
I never know when it will come on, I can be at home in the most relaxed
atmosphere, sipping natural spring water, no stress, no fuss, and then
wham! like a shot gun.: stomach time is here again.then i can play 100
shows in a row,guzzle boric acid and do a load of television interviews,
results: not even a burp. This has left doctors with no ideas except the
usual, "Here Kurdt, try another peptic ulcer pill and lets jam this fibre-
optic tube with a video camera on its end down your throat for the third
time.(called an ENDOSCOPE)and see whats going on in there. yep, your in
pain. the stomach lining is extremely red and inflamed. this could be
life threatening. try eating ice cream from now on. Please lord!
to hell with hit records, let me have my very own unexplainable, rare,
stomach disease named after me. The title of our next double concept album
could be called "COBAINS DISEASE". A rock opera all about vomiting gastric
juices,being a borderline annorexic-Auschwitz-grunge-boy. And with this
epic, an accompanying ENDOSCOPE rock video.
I am the product of seven months of screaming at the top of my lungs almost
every night. seven months of jumping around like a retarded rheesus monkey.
seven months of answering the same questions over and over. The cherub,
little scruff youve grown to know from the back of the nevermind album
is proof that film adds ten pounds to your body, because ive been the same
bird weight since ive had the dreaded gut rot. Well ive spewed enough,
probably too much but oh well. for every one opinionated,pissy,self-appointed
rock judge-cermudgeon, theres a thousand screaming teenagers.
hope i die before i turn into Pete Townshend.

mr advice

and others like him

this

WomBan

DE_JA VOO- DOO   BY: KurDt Kobain

stomach bile

An industrial size garbage sack filled with liquid demerol,
sweet cutgrass juice, the urine of extremely retarded,fetal alcohol syn
syndrome victims from Costa Mesa who are one chromosone away from severely
dangerous examples of why we will become a third world country in a matter
of years. If this is the current state of the underground,youth culture
Id rather retire to my big mansion petting my pot bellied pig,eating Hagen
Dahs ice cream with this garbage sack I.V. , in an iron lung deprevation
tank,submerged in a glassno no a gold aquarium filled with epsom salts
with full visibility of a television monitor projecting endless footage
of fishing and golfing programs with the grateful dead pumped through
the speaker. Relaxing , lying naked except for a tie dyed T- shirt dyed
with the urine of Phil Collins and the blood of Cherry Garcia,
Ill be so relaxed and famous that an old man named Bob will travel miles
to visit me. He will pull apart my pyles and stick it in. He will die
just as he comes inside of me and all of his orgones and bad thoughts
and desires for truth will soak into the walls of my lower intestines.
I will be re-fueled. so re-fueled as to work up the energy to run on
foot to the grave of Leadbelly, dig up his corpse and put us on a one
way ticket to the Vatican. I will nail the corpse of Huddie in a corner
of the ceiling, paint him white and decorate him with costume jewelry.

Womben

Womban

its so relieving to know that your leaving
as soon as you get paid

its so relaxing to know that your asking

its so   soothing to know that youll sue me
whenever you get the chance

its so religious

She eyes me like a pisces - when I am weak
I've been buried in your heart shaped box for weeks
I've been drawn into your magnet tar pit trap
I wish I could eat your cancer when you
    turn black

Hey - wait - I've got a new complaint
  for ever in debt to your priceless advice
Hate - wait - *   "

She fries me like cold Ice cream - headaches and chills
                   I'll cook my own Meals

uncertainty   certainty

I wish there was someone I could ask for advice,
someone who wouldn't make me feel like a creep
for spilling my guts and trying to explain all
the insecurities that have plagued me for oh, about 25
years now.   I wish someone could explain to me
why exactly I have no desire to learn any more,
why I used to have so much energy and the need
to search for miles and weeks for anything new
and different. excitement.   I was once a magnet
for attracting new offbeat personalities who would
introduce me to music and books that of the
obscure and I would soak it into my system
like a rabid sex crazed junkie hyperactive mentally retarded
toddler who's just had her first taste of sugar.   This weeks
obsession, vagina medical books, the meat puppets and

Lester Bangs

why in the hell do journalists insist
on ~~creating~~ coming up with
a second rate freudian evaluation on my
lyrics when they 90 % of the time
they've transcribed ~~them incorrectly~~ the lyrics incorrectly ?

there are more bad ^{Rock} journalists than
there are bad ^{Rock} bands
~~does anyone remember~~
what the fuck do they teach
journalists at school anyway ?
~~to~~ what do they use as
I would have reference or examples ?
printed the lyrics
on the sleeve of
the album if I   does anyone remember lester bangs.
knew it would be
such I'm giving you factual quotes from my mind
a problem I'm fed up with having a long winded 2 hour
with
people discussions with journalists and finding ~~they~~
that they've chosen all the unimportant more
tabloid esque quotes of the past 2 hours.
Rock bands are at the mercy of
the journalist and in my opinion there
is not one I can think of who deserves
to own a pen.

you probably need more qualifications to
be a welder than a ~~journalist~~ to get
a job being a journalist.

thanks for your second rate freudian
evaluation on my ~~present state~~ minds present
state of "oh gee I feel guilty for
not expecting to sell so many records."

Ask my friends ; Ive always been this skinny
You know me from pictures, film adds ten pounds
to a person. Youve never seen me before in real
life until that most memorable night.

I suffer from narcolepsy ; I suffer from
bad sleeping and eating habits. I suffer
from being on tour for 7 fucking months.

Sometimes I wonder if I~~could~~ could be the very well
luckiest boy in the world.
For some reason I've been blessed with
loads of ~~neat~~ stuff within the past year and I don't really
think these baubles and gifts ~~I have been acquired~~ by
the fact that im a critically acclaimed, internationally
beloved teen Idol, demi-god like blonde front man,
cryptically honest, stuttering, outspoken speech impediment
articulate~~ly~~ award acceptance speech, Golden boy,
Rock star who has finally, finally
come out of the closet in regards to his vicious
2 month drug habit, showering the world with ~~and~~ the
~~greatest~~ classic I can no longer keep this a
secret because it pains me to hide any part
of my private life from my adoring, concerned,
we think of you as our public domain, cartoon character
but we still love you fans Yes my children
in the words of a total fuckin geek ~~we~~ speaking
in behalf of all the world " We really appreciate you
finally admitting what we have been accusing
you of, we needed to hear it because we were
concerned because the Katty Gossip ~~and~~ jokes
and speculation at our jobs schools and parties had
become well uh, exhausted oh yeah the bitter,
pissy reincarnation of Pick yer King has strayed
from the positive introduction. so heres the
things I've had the wonderful opportunity to have acquired,
the wonderful people I've met and the things people
have said to me that I look back upon and hold dear to my heart.
1st while in ~~loudly~~ England in ~~June~~ June I went to
Rough Trade records where I make my pathetic annual,
effort to find the 1st raincoats album

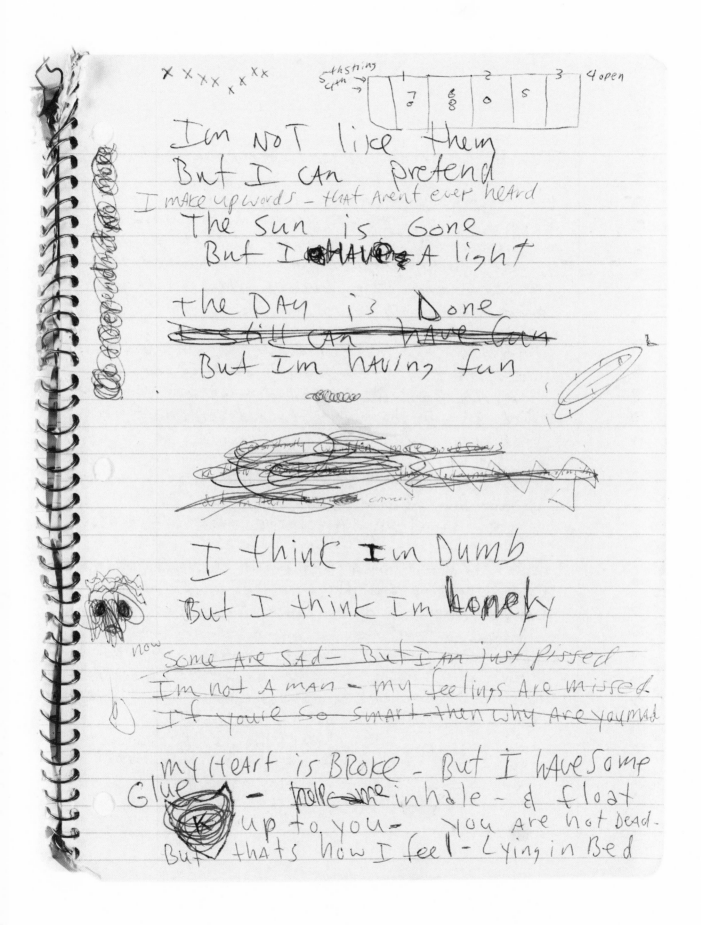

I'm NOT like them
But I can pretend
I make up words — that aren't ever heard
The sun is Gone
But I ~~Have~~ A light

the DAY is Done
~~still can Have fun~~
But I'm having fun

I think I'm Dumb

But I think I'm ~~lonely~~

now
~~Some Are Sad — But I'm just pissed~~
~~I'm not A man — my feelings Are missed~~
~~If you're so smart — then why Are you mad~~

my Heart is Broke — But I have some
Glue — ~~hold me~~ inhale — & float
up to you — you are not dead.
But that's how I feel — Lying in Bed

193

I'd be better off if i kept my mouth shut.

But theres a cool breeze chapping my lips
As my jaw hangs open discharging waterfalls
of guilty drool. My eyes are pinned and the stupid
fucking British press bought the lie that I
suffer from narcolepsy.   Yeah, talkin bout
drugs. opening my mouth for the disaffected youth
to ask them a question.   Are you gay?
bisexual? A bigot? A redneck? A prom queen?
A porn star? A topless dancer? did you know the
King, the king of Rockn Roll Elvis Presley
died in the bathroom face down, pants down,
choking on blue shag carpet with the remainder
of his stool proudly ~~~~~~ sticking out of his
big fat Ass?   Are you kinda mad sometimes
At your mom or dad kinda, in a way?
        I went on A three week Heroine
Binge after our last European tour, got a little
habit, kicked it in A Hotel in three days (sleeping
Kicking, vomiting and the worst gas youll ever
know. then 3 days later we went on A
Australian tour And on to Japan during which I
collected A very distressing stomach disorder,
went to A doctor and he gave me stomach
pills that Ive had before and didn't work and
some five milligram methadone tablets.
        They stopped the stomach pains, I ran out
when I got home then went to A hospital
for A few days to recover from that.
        More bad gas.

~~Now I don't do drugs anymore~~

Yeah, I went on A 3 week drug binge and now
I'm thought of ~~as an~~ emaciated, yellow skinned, Zombie like ~
~ Evil drug fiend, Junky, ~~dope~~ lost cause, on the
brink of Death, Self destructive, selfish pig,
A loser who shoots up in the back stage ~~area~~ just seconds before
~~going on~~ a performance

I tried heroine the first time in 1987 in aberdeen and proceeded
to use it about 10 more times from 87 to 90. when I got
back form our Second European Tour with Sonic Youth I
decided to use heroine on a daily basis because of an ongoing
stomach ailment that I had been suffering from for the past
five years had literally taken me to the point of wanting to
kill myself. For five years every Single day of my life.
Every time I swallowed a piece of food I would experience
an excruciating burning nauseous pain in the upper part of
my stomach lining. The pain became even more severe on tour
due to lack of a proper and regimented eating schedule and diet.
&Since th beginning of this disorder I~~ve~~ had 10 upper and
lower Gastrointestinal proceedures wich found an enflamed irritation
in the same place. I ~~tried to~~ consulted 15 different doctors and
tried about 50 different types of ulcer medication. The only thing
I found that worked were heavy opiates. There were many times
that I found myself literally incapacitated in bed for weeks
vomiting and starving. So I decided ~~If~~ I feel like a junky
as it is so I may as well be one. After the last European
tour I vowed to never go on tour again unless my condition
is either masked or cured. I did heroine for about one
month then found myself realicing that I wouldnt be able to
get drugs when ~~oo~~ we go to ~~japan in~~ Australia and Japan
so Courtney and I detoxed in a Hotel room

I went to Australia and of course the stomach pain started immediately. We had to cancel a few shows because the pain left me immobile doubled up on the bathroom floor vomiting water and blood. I was literally starving to death. My weight was down to about 110 lbs. I was taken to a doctor at the advice of my management who gave me physeptone. ~~later noticed~~ The pills seemed to work better than anything else I've tried. a bit later into the tour I read the fine print on the bottle it read: "physeptone - contains methadone!" Hooked again. We survived Japan but by that time opiates and touring had started to take their toll on my body. and I wasn't in much better health than I was off of drugs.

I returned home to find that country had gotten hooked again so we checked ~~he~~ into a detox center for 2 weeks. She recovered. I instantly regained that familiar burning nausea and decided to ~~either~~ kill myself or ~~to~~ stop the pain. I bought a gun but chose drugs instead. I stayed on heroine until one month before frances due date. again I checked into a detox center and went through 2 months of the slowest process I have ever witnessed in recovery 60 days of starvation and vomiting. Hooked to an IV and moaning out loud with the worst stomach pain I have ever experienced. By the last 2 weeks I was introduced to a medicine called buprenorphine which I found eleviates the pain within minutes. It has been used experimentally in a few detox centers for opiate and cocaine withdrawal. The best thing about it is that there are no known side effects. ~~and~~ It acts as an opiate but it doesn't get you high. I've been on an increasingly smaller dose of it for nine months and havent had a single stomach episode since. The potency range of beprenorphine is that like a mild barbiturate on a scale of 1 to 10 its a 1 and heroine is 10.
of

Dear Empty TV
the Entity of all Corporate
GODS.
how fucking dare you embrace
such trash journalism from an
overweight, unpopular at highschool,
Cow who severely needs her karma
Broken. My lifes Dedication
is NOW TO Do Nothing
But SLAG MTV and
LYNN Herschberg
who by the way is in kahoots with
her lover kurt Loder (Gin blossom drunk)!

We will survive without

you. easily
the oldschool is going
DOWN FAST
JUST FACE
IT

Kurdt
Kobain
professional
Rock musician

199

4 month media blackout

use just once and destroy
invasion of our piracy
after birth of a nation
starve without your skeleton key

③ ✗ I love you for what I am not
   ✗ I did not want what I have got
④ ✗ blanket acned with cigarette burns
     speak at once while taking turns

① ✗ this has nothing to do with what you think
   ✗ If you ever think at all
   ~~revolutionary debris~~
   ~~litters the floor of wall street~~

what is what I need — what is wrong with me
what is what I need — what do I think I
think

use use your enemies
and save save your friends   Bridge
and find find your place
and spit spit the truth

② ✗ Bi polar opposites attract
   ✗ All of a sudden my water broke
     free ~~xeroxes~~ for all alternateens
③ ✗ second rate word by pass throat
                        of ferns

Hes such a knob

9 month media
BLACKOUT

I love you my lovely dear
I dont want you any where

I want you to be my bride
no not really, I just lied

Will you love me with your might
I'll beat you an inch from your life

                    AWAY
hold me tight with breaths of truths
I wish a terminal disease on you

Gosh I feel so darn confused
ever felt like youve been used ?

Bi-polar opposites attract

All of a sudden my water broke

I love you for what Im not

primary
→ second rate word play bypass throat throat

Bypass
Use once and destroy
invasion of our piracy
afterbirth of a nation
blanket acned with cigarette
I forget what I look like to you burns

starve without your skeleton key

201

A matter of opinion

Second RATE
third Generation

Personal Preference

A
Date
With
FusioN

Raw Power ⎫ the
Funhouse ⎬ Stooges
the Stooges ⎭

Generic Flipper – Flipper
Surfer Rosa – Pixies
Trompe le Monde – Pixies
Pod – Breeders
VAselines pink EP
Aerosmith – Rocks
Gang of four – entertainment
Nevermind the Bullocks – Sex pistols
Flowers of Romance – PIL
Jamboree – Beat Happening
Superfuzz Big Muff – Mudhoney
Leadbellys lAst session – Hudie Ledbetter
LAnd shark – Fang
Millions of dead Cops – MDC
Damaged – Black flag
Scratchacid EP – scratchacid
Locust abortion Technician – butthole surfers
Rock for light – Bad Brains
Raincoats – Raincoats
Philosophy of the World – shaggs
Combat Rock – clash
Are we not men – Devo
B-52s
Collosal Youth – Young Marble Giants
Kleenex
Slits – Slits
Daydream Nation – Sonic Youth
man who sold the World – David Bowie
GI – Germs

Saccharine Trust – EP
Get the Knack – the Knack
Atomizer – Big black
Great expectations – Jadfair
Is this Real ⎬ Wipers
Youth of America ⎭
Love Rubbing the impossible to burst – Hussy Bear
XtC

Jackie 362.0610

M. Carrodus—
"Squadron Formation
King."
TEBALA MOTORCYCLE CORPS
TEBALA TEMPLE A A O N M S
Rockford, Illinois
This unit participates in Shrine and Civic Parades.
Performs in Precision Maneuvers

QP 549

Tel (415) 986-8866

1441 Grant, San Francisco, CA 94133

Hi Ian and Nikki,
Happy New year, Merry Xmas
Happy Halloween, Happy VAlentines
day, Happy Thanksgiving,
HAPPY Birthday, maybe
Sometime next year I could
Squeeze my friends into my
Rock-schedule and we all
Could go Shriner Bowling.
Love Kurdt

QUANTITY POSTCARDS
Mfr./Pub./Wholesale/Retail/Mail Order

Catalogue
available

©1987 Quantity Postcards

SWINGERS

ALICIA OSTRIKER

Passing that fiery tree—if only she could

Be making love,
Be making poetry,
Be exploding, be speeding through the univers

Like a photon, like a shower
Of yellow blazes—7

Mead

Flipper

washed up, has been, drug addicts.

70 sheets/college ruled
11x8½in/27.9x21.6cm

notebook

06540   © 1985 The Mead Corporation, Dayton, Ohio 45463 U.S.A.

$ 3-19

0 43100 06540 1

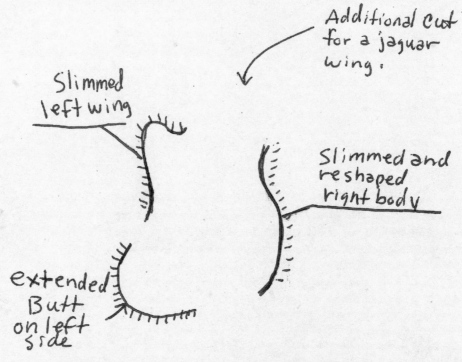

Additional cut
for a jaguar
wing.

Slimmed
left wing

Slimmed and
reshaped
right body

extended
Butt
on left
side

This is a mustang ~~cut~~ cut differently
with a few inches added to the wing
and left side of butt and the left
wing and side cut thinner

mustang/Jaguar
Jagstang

LEFT HANDED

very thin neck
small fret
wire

white tortoise
shell pick Guard

mustang Single coils
& electronics

Double coil
pickup

whatever
bridge & tailpiece
works best

Tune o matic
Bridge

Hot double coil
Back Pickup

Not sure what kind yet

Probably 59 Les Paul

Dots

Arched
Headstock

Jaguar
front Pickup

or just A Simple
Jaguar neck
and Headstock

Schaller
tuners

208

mustang Pickup

Hot RAil

3-WAY
Pickup
Push Button

Vol

Tone

Humbucker

Color: Same old blue/green/aqua
from the mustang

If this Headstock isn't possible,
then the old Fender headstock will
be fine.

LEFT HANDED!®

Jaguar front
Pick up

Cream colored
tortoise shell

double coil
Pickup
Preferably Sq'les paul

preferably jaguar tailpiece
and tune o matic bridge
or whatever is simplest

mustang guts switches

Convexed/
curve on
Back

Kurt Kobain model
1993

c/o Gold Mountain ent
Cahuenga blvd ~~E~~ west
Suite 450 LA CA 90068

michael meisel/John Silva

211

with the phrasing I allow myself it isn't very easy to
be ~~lyrically~~ lyrically prolific

~~Dike Girls~~

Boys write songs for girls - what a simple world
how the hell do I - know whats on inside
what else should I say? - All my words are grey
what else could I write? - I'm sorry I am white

Such an easy thing - such a shiny ring
let me grow some breasts - I cheated on my test
I dont have ~~the~~ the right - to say whats on your mind
your not allowed to sing - All Apologies

In the sun in the sun I feel As one in the sun
in the sun I'm married and buried

you have every right - to want to start a fight
~~treated like a dog~~
~~its gone on too long - treated like their dogs~~
~~such an easy thing - let my sister sing~~
what else can I do? - I'm in love with you

Seven months ago I chose to put myself in a position ~~s~~ which requires the highest form of responsibility a person can have. A responsibility ~~of which~~ that ~~should not be~~ should not be dictated ~~by thinking that I should~~ rather ~~want to~~ take on this responsibility. ~~Every~~ Everytime I see a television show that has dying children or seeing a testimonial by a parent who recently lost their child I can't help but cry. The thought of losing my baby haunts me every day.

I'm even a bit unnerved to take her in the car in fear of getting into an accident. I swear that If I ever been in it. the divorce find myself in a similar situation than Youve ~~been~~ I will fight to ~~my~~ death to keep the right to provide for my child. I'll go out of my way to remind her that I love her more ~~than~~ I love myself. not because it's a fathers duty but because I want to out of love. And If Courtney and I end up hating eachothers guts we both will be adult and responsible enough to be pleasant to one another when our child is around us.

I know ~~that~~ youve felt for years that my mother has somehow brainwashed Kim and I into hating you, ~~when~~ I cant stress enough how totally untrue this is and I think its a very lazy and lame excuse to use for not trying harder to provide your fatherly duties, I cant recall my mother ever talking shit about you until much later in the game, right around the last two years of Highschool. That was a time when I came to my own realizations without the need of my mothers input. Yet she ~~took the~~ noticed my contempt for you and your family and acted upon my feelings in accordance by taking the opportunity to vent her frustrations out on you. Everytime she talked shit about you Ive let her know that I don't appreciate it and how unnecessary I think it is. I've never taken sides with you or my mother because while I was growing up I had equal contempt for you both.

MR Producer

try to find oak or maple sheets to be nailed on rough plywood

UTENCILS: five 5ft x 5ft pieces of plywood. thickness depends on type of wood. preferrably ½ inch thick. Carpeted on one side each. Thick, dense carpet is preferred.

__Guitar:__ RCA ribbon mics

looking for a transducer element

Beyer 160 - 130

BK-5 ?

With Beyer 4 to 6 inches close to amp. no closer or static breakage will result.

Setting: the closer to the cabinet the bassier with most other brands.

Amp Settings: ① try mids on full.
② try Highs at lower than usual setting.
③ Lows full.

EFFects: slight compression.
Room chamber
Alesis is very small dimensions

carpeted Plywood

④ Use carpeted Cabinet.
⑤ build or use A large cardboard box for muffle chamber, or pieces of plywood with Carpet to make an enclosure around the cabinet. allowing at least 2 feet of breathing space

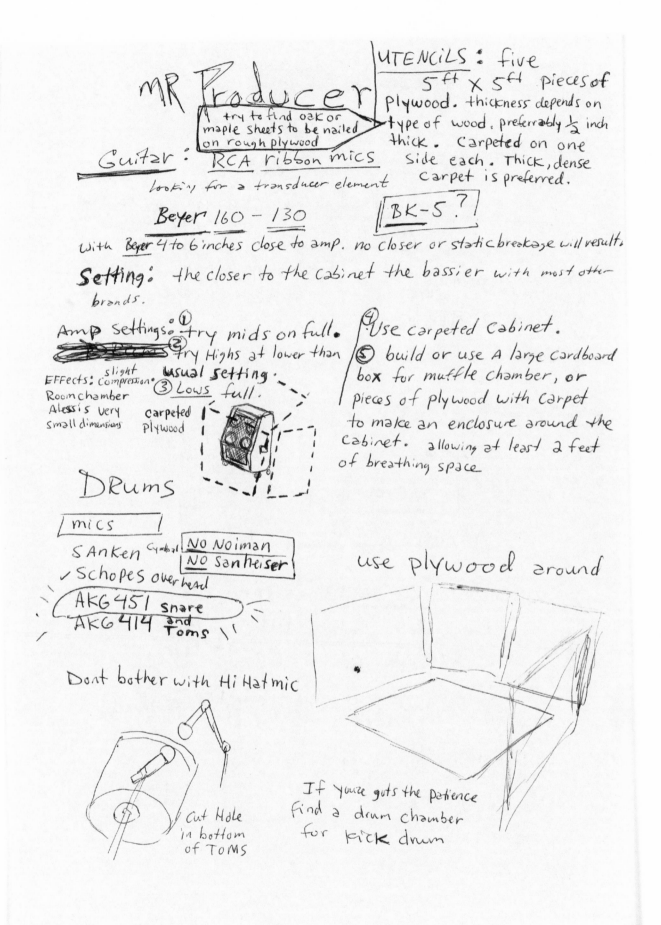

DRums

| mics |

S Anken Cymbal
✓ Schopes overhead
AKG 451 snare
AKG 414 and Toms

NO Noiman
NO Sanheiser

Dont bother with Hi Hat mic

use plywood around

Cut Hole in bottom of TOMS

If youre guts the patience find a drum chamber for Kick drum

New ideas
for Mevins

[put mics inside Toms]

record dale with cymbals
Heavily taped so they make
No Noise! this will allow us
to use the room mics A lot louder
then dub cymbals crashes later.

put Three mics on the snare
one of them will be recorded
Very Very hot to the point of
distirtion After about 4 dbs

And 2 more room mics
besides the little schapers room
mics About 3 feet Away
from kick And snares

more chorus on BAss guitar.

use very directional mics for this

217

IAn
mcclAY

NIRVANA

I hate myself and I want to die

1. Serve the servants
2. Scentless apprentice
3. Heart shaped Box
4. Penny royal tea

D G C C$

David Geffin

Sup Pop   SUP POP

5. Frances farmer will/ have her revenge ON Seattle

6. Eustacian tube turrets
7. * Dumb
8. Rape me
9. Very ape
10. Milk it

Produced by
A dick in the
Snow feb 12-26
1993
Personnel:
Mr Pissy: Guitar/mouth
Suavy Smooth: Bass
Jocko Accidente:
Polyrythims

11. Four month media blackout
12. Verse chorus Verse
13. * La La La (Alternateen anthem) Dotin chetto *

Hi Simon,

Thanks A load for the drawings, pictures and music. They're the best presents I've ~~gotten~~ recieved in a really long time!

I looove the stinky puffs! and would love to hear more once you all record some more. I was wondering if you would be interested in drawing some pictures for the cover of the next NIRVANA record wich will be ready to sell once we have the artwork done. I think you draw really good and ⟶ (over)

It would mean a lot to me if you'd consider it. heres some ideas I had.

NIRVANA

I hate myself and I want to die

(DAVE ← or → chris n kurt

whatever you want

It would be great if you drew about 5 or more or less so we have plenty to choose between.

the title of the album is rather negative but kind of funny. Its called:

I hate myself and I want to die.

Heres some info that needs to be written for the back of the LP
DAVE - drums. chris-bass. kurt Geetar-n-mouth.
D.G.C records and subpop. recorded by steve albini.
Cello on LALALA & dumb oh, and Artwork
by simon Timony | Well, bye write back soon
Love kurdt Hi Jad! &

Since my freshly found relationships with employees of the *corporate ogre
corporate *(catch phrase © copyright Calvin Johnson) I've found realized learned that there are
of Beat Happening
a handful of very honorable and sincere ♪ music lovers who are posing as the enemy
to infiltrate the mechanics of the Empire, to help destroy what we all have known for
oriented garbage
too long as shit Rock, prefabricated, incestually politically business; a smoke
the no using A
screen of Honesty and true talent and to keep it will willing to Kiss Ass at risk of
to clog the arteries of those
unchallenging,
and most importantly
undeserving
At the top
of the Heap.

1	Sonic Youth - Goo	
2	Every good boy deserves fudge - Mudhoney	
3	Bandwagonesque - Teenage fanclub	
4	Trompe Le Monde - Pixies	
5	Beat Happening - dreamy	
X 6	Violent femmes - why do birds sing?	
X 7	Bull Head - melvins	
8	Strangely Beautiful EP Television personalities	
9	Army of Lovers - Pretty little Baka Guy reissue - Shonen knife	
10	Item out of time Hole - pretty on inside	
	No 1 Single - crucified - Army of Lovers	

the Heap
of Dung.
The Heap starts with
the Ass kissers to all the way
up to the top where the
old school
cherry or music
Publication sits
looking down
on the
Baby Birds
with eyes still shut,
and feeding them
dehydrated worms.
But as I said before
the small percent of
deserving bands and music
loving employees will keep
sawing away at the Heap
and if we fail we will just
simply wait until the
cherry rots of old
Age
and we will
use your historical
decomposition
as a
reference
or a sweaty
bed time story

1. Sonic youth - Goo - |DGC|
2. Mudhoney - Every good boy deserves fudge - |Sub Pop|
3. Pixies - Trompe le Monde - |Elektra|
4. Teen age fanclub - Bandwagonesque - |DGC|
5. Hole - pretty on the inside - |Caroline|
6. Beat Happening - dreamy - |Sub Pop|
7. Television personalities - strangely beautiful EP - |Fire records|
8. Shonen Knife - Pretty little Baka Guy (reissue) |Zero| (Japanese import)
9. Melvins - Bullhead - |Boner|
10. Violent femmes - why do birds sing?

P.S. Urge Overkill - Supersonic storybook - |Touch-n-Go|
No 1 Single: Army of Lovers - crucified

As remembrance
of a warning to
nextime, plant our seeds
closer to a cleaner
Asshole.

You have failed at conditioning
the young ones of the underworld
whom you have spawned,
and you yourselves are
aborted should have
been Ichenex
or poached fried or scrambled sperm.
or neutered eggs.

Serve the servants

Initially this song was about 'coming of age' during a time where your old enough to support yourself without the aid of your parents. A theme for the twenty somethings, if you will not. Ive always felt that a person doesnt necessarily have to force themselves to love their parents simply because of blood. If you don't like your parents or relatives, dont fake it tell them how you feel and in my own way I decided to let my father know that I dont hate him. I simply dont have anything to say and I don't need a father son relationship with a person whom I dont want to spend Christmas with. In other words: I love you. I don't hate you. I dont want to talk to you.

^A Boring

Scentless apprentice

~~was about record?~~ ~~read the line~~ "perfume" by Patrick Susskind

Heart shaped box ~~revised~~

Camille's ~~flower/vagina theory~~ vaginal/flower theory bleeding and spreading into ~~fabric~~ the fabric that leonardo would have used to ~~invent the~~ improve ~~the his~~ ~~hang glider~~ hang glider but he died before he could change the course of history. shit. I Claudius I play dumb for thee! and dorothy and toto (the dog) not the band. and rusty Pyles. ~~The fem~~ The male Seahorse empragnates the female Seahorse, she ~~carries them~~ holds them through most of the developmental stages then transferes the babies to the father who carries them through the last stages ~~then~~ gives them birth. ~~They share~~ ~~das transformation~~ and finally
The majority of our so called Outlaw heroes of the old west were nothing but fucked up psychopath ~~Sympathisers ex~~ Confederate soldiers. Sympathisers of the way it used to be with alcohol fuled ^Bi polar ~~internal~~ rage during the transformation years. killing every darkie they could find. Heroes my ass! ~~clear and stop~~ If I only had a heart. ~~I don't~~ listen you snivelling little, opinionated, spoiled punts, H I dont hate you. I love you. Ah god it feels so good to be clean DR Bronner.
Kinda like when Axl ~~was~~ was butt naked in that epic video of his.

Rape me

How Bold ~~should the print be~~ shall ~~I make the print~~ the print be made?

~~in order to help you in the simple pleasure of reading?~~ ~~so questions~~

OBvious. oblivious. settle down. calm. calm. its ok. sshh.
Hold still. Sshh. Hold still.

Frances farmer will have her revense on Seattle

The conspirators are still alive and well in their comfortable, warm, safe home's.
gag on her ashes. jag on her gash. uh, god is ⊕ A woman and she's
~~Black~~. BACK in Black

Dumb

All that pot. all that supposedly unaddictive, harmless, safe
reefer that damaged my nerves and ruined my memory and made
me feel like wanting to ~~kill~~ blow up the prom. and the patience
to play guitar for 5 hours every day after school. and to sleep
during the day when I should have paid a bit more attention
to my studies. especially in English sometimes an A+ sometimes
an X on my hand or forehead and the feeling that it just
wasnt ever strong enough so I climbed the ladder to the
poppie. Not everyone does the latter so Ive learned one lesson.
I have absolutely no right to express my opinions until I
know all the answers. far out.

Very ape

I forget.

penny royal tea

An ~~abortive~~ herbal abortive.
it doesnt work you hippie.

Radio friendly unit shifter

Boy this will really get the A&R mans Blood boiling.
Hell be so Pissed. heh heh. Clever.
getting into the inner me. self indulgent.
way out there - ~~bdae~~.

~~the total day live through Sub~~

Ask about Dantes Inferno movie from the 30's
to use instead of ~~making~~ our own props
we will use the scenes of people intwined old withering oak trees

Sebadoh

Alex wages

tourrets
    me . old man .   ~~he made~~
have made my conclusion. but nobody will listen anymore.

  Birds. Birds are and always have been reincarnated old men
with tourrets syndrome ~~out every morning~~ having somehow managed
to ~~earn~~ the reproductive saga ~~and~~ they fuck eachother and
  dupe
tend to their home repairs and children while never missing
their true mission. to scream at the top of their lungs
in horrified hellish rage every morning at day break
to warn us all of the truth. they know the truth.
Screaming bloody murder all over the world in our ears
but sadly we dont speak bird.
  the whales respond ~~in a similar way~~ with their message for
us in similar ways. by beaching themselves

    this album is dedicated to dead relatives.
      they arepwarm and full of happy smiles.
        SAfe

All apologies

Nothing has or will
Nothing could or should
Alternateens ignoring the Budweiser sponsor banner behind the 10 yrs +
Acts.
An excuse to get laid
~~Kurt toder and talk the open are complete~~
Jimmy Carter was ~~was~~ and still is an extremely
loving and sensible man. but when I was a kid
I only remember that he liked peanuts and had big lips.

milk it

If you really love me you will send medical supplies.
oh god, he's awake again. don't look. just ignore it. before
he starts to. oh shh. he fell asleep again. thank God.
How do you feel? Shhh be quiet.

A multitude

Serve ~~the~~ servants

Oh lord. the guilt of sucksess. ~~was~~ during the past
two years I have slowly come to the conclusion that I do
not want to die. ~~no~~ I am now no more of a recluse
than I used to be. I lived in the Ⓚ kingdom for a few
years hiding in a little apartment. ~~could~~ And now I stand in
my room without a sandbox ~~so I don't rather~~ on punk Rock show
attendant ratio I would say it's about the same. I am still
equally annoyed and equally impressed with the same old familiar
ritual of standing in a room full of people hoping to feel a
vibration that runs through my back when I hear a familiar
song or see an enigmatic performance from ~~so~~ ~~chose~~ A
collection of people who choose to strap on pieces of wood
which are electrically activated and manipulated
Ive never claimed to be a punk rocker.
I was inspired by it, as much as Led Zeppelin or Aerosmith

& the beatles ~~etc..~~ but oh lord never paul pleeease!
Is it egotistical to talk about myself like this?
I guess this song is for my father who is incapable of
communicating at a level of affection in which I have always
expected

Nordic trAc

1-800 382 9177

Augment ensamble

verile

Kevlar

Kevin & Co for the Long form

~~On Anurysm~~

~~On Anurysm: keep the Audio from the Amsterdam show but keep the edits from out the same.~~

1 ON Anurysm: Keep Amsterdam audio when first change happens ie· kurdt in over coat

2 Take out Dave & Chris playin Aerosmith song

3 Put Subtitle in "Bronchitis" flashing throughout Dive

4 Video footage of us with Jason "the early years) put in sub title = Jason everman guitar Chad channing drums Rhino Records LA 88. Song. Sifting

5 Cut out the last half of dave talking about new bands

6 Start my rant just as I say Black flag flipper ~~then finish the rest~~ leave the rest.

sub 7 Rock star lesson: ~~sing out of tune your guitar is~~ title = [for Come As U are] when your guitar is out of tune, sing out of tune along with it

~~The one~~

8 Englands prestigious Top of the pops equivalent of US's American Bandstand.

Cut to 1st IN Bloom video we did with one camera in dresses destroying the set.

9 Replace mollys lips with Reading version with ~~Eugene~~ singing

Add the scene where I hand the guitar to the audience. I think its from Reading

And the penis and flower petal face in camera. ~~the~~ performance piece kurdt does in Rio.

~~the first Vinyl Rele~~
but the video's recorded Audio version will
be the re-mixed one.

---

① release Albini version: mastered — different sequence under title:
"I Hate myself and want to die."
on VinyL LP, cassette and 8-track ← Yes! Yes! Yes!
Albini producer, mixologist credits. with sticker that says: NIRVANAS
Latest studio release. for 93' contains Heart shaped box, Rape me & 12 others.
Retail: Sold to small mom and pop stores or anywhere vinyl can be found.
NO-PROMOS sent out!!!

② one month later: after many lame reviews and reports
On the curmudgeonly, uncompromising vinyl, cass, 8-track only release.
We Release the Re-mixed ~~version~~ & re-recorded ~~of~~ bass and acoustic
guitar version under the title "Verse Chorus Verse." on Vinyl LP, cassette,
and God forbid, Cd. with sticker that says: This Album is the radio-
friendly, unit shifting, compromise Version which, by the way, NIRVANA is
extremely proud of. Contains Heart shaped box, Rape me & 10 more.

③ Release video of Heart shaped box at the same time of the 1st
vinyl, cass, 8-track only release. but the re-mix audio version will accompany
it.

Hi, im the moody, bohemian member
of the group. blonde frontman.
the sensetive artist type.
I like: pasta, turtles, girls with weird eyes,
writing, reading, keeping my mouth shut,
cake decorating, horseback riding, gun cleaning,
Sally Struthers impersonations, pina coladas
and getting caught in the rain, buttfucking,
accupuncture, painting, friends, cats, goats,
mo-hair sweaters, cultivating a fine army of
facial blemishes, scarification, playing music with
my band, my ~~girlfriend~~ wife, ~~and~~ my family and all of
the people with whom our band works with.
I would only wear a tie died T shirt if it were made from the

Blood of Gerry Garcia
and the urine of Phil Collins,

the vaselines, the breeders, the Stooges, the pixies, sex pistols,
raincoats, melvins, tales of terror, scratch acid, butthole surfers,
young marble giants, urge overkill, marine girls, Jesus lizard, Teenage fanclub
slits, mud honey, Beat happening, Cramps, Shonen knife, Delta 5
Sonic youth, Black flag, R.e.m, meat puppets II, witchy poo, Hole,
TV personalities, Daniel Johnston, the Sonics, lead belly, the wipers,
Half Japanese, Dead moon, public enemy, Big Black, the ~~knack~~, Germs,
Husker Du, Dinosaur Jr, Captain America, saints, velvet underground,
Lee Hazlewood, Hank williams, flipper, feederz, Lewd, Bad Brains,
Patsy Cline, Devo, Clash, ~~Dead~~ Fear, Army of Lovers,
fugazi, ~~(circled out)~~ Bikini kill, ~~(circled out)~~
Beatnik Termites, the staple Singers, Discharge, Cannanes, Bratmobile, Saccharine trust,
Dirt, pavement, love child, Superchunk, Boredoms, Sebadoh, Axemen, Cows →

Shocking Blue
wire,

Here Are
Some of the
BAnds I
like.

Leonard Cohen,
PYLon B-52's
Duh, Didjits
Mazzy star
Sun city Girls   TK records
Calamity Jane   Sprinkler
Tinklers, some
Velvet sidewalk
         Smegma
         Go team
Rites of spring
VoiD shop
Assistants
Nip Drivers,

229

Fire records
339 seven sisters RD
London N15 Grd England

Suck dog
PO Bx 1491 Dover NH, 03820

MATB
Simple machines
Po Box 10290 Arlington VA
22210-1290

independent labels ~~address~~
90260

SST: po box 1 Lawndale CA K Seminal twang
25520 Chicago IL 60625   Box   Olympia WA
Touch and Go   7154 K 98507   Sympathy for the record industry
                           130

Boner, matador, **Sub pop**, ecstatic peace   BASATANKA Rockville

Kill rock stars, feel good all over, Homestead 4-AD

Rough Trade Caroline C/D presents   T/K records Alternative Tentacles
out of Business 114 West 26th st   42423 Portland Oregon
              NY, NY 10001   97242   Twin Tone

music publications: fact sheet five.

CAll Thurston FANZINES: Bikini kill Alternative Press   Jigsaw INK Disease Your flesh

Girl germs, flip side, maximum Rock n roll

murder can be fun, Spin, forced exposure,

Amok Research, Option, Kitten Kore, And she's not even pretty.

Technicolor effect for film.

Old weathered man in hospital bed with a rubber foetus in his IV Bottle chris dave and I sitting at the foot of the bed, impatiently waiting for him to pass away. In the hospital room the curtains are drawn 90% of the way with a blinding white light shooting through the curtains. Lots of flowers in the room and kurdt hold an old pocket watch dangling back and forth — indicating that time is running out.

4 year old aryan girl with bright blonde hair with vivid blue eyes. in a klu klux klan robe on sitting in a small shack. the walls of the shack is covered with stargazer lillies with stems cut off and the butt end of the flowers and glued on the every where on the walls. Each flower has a bright light alluminating each of them. from behind them. Another shot of the little girl holding hands with an elder. he squeezes her hand as if she could never escape. bright red blood soaks in from inside of the girls robe. Close up of red ink or blood soaking in to white fabric then a gust of wind blows her kkk hat off, the camera follows it through blowing above a field of poppies. Eventually the hat turns into a butterfly net and chases butterflies through out the field. then it falls into a small pool of black tar (india ink. another closeup of black ink-goo soaks into the white fabric. then we see after the hat is completely black it appears to be a black witches hat and blows away with a gust of wind.

~~old man on a cross~~

Old weathered interesting looking man on a cross with black crows on his arms, pecking at his face — Scarecrow/Jesus.

Animation, forest Dantes inferno from the thirties
          Bodies entwined in old oak trees
          maybe we can use the original
          footage from that movie

Optical illusion

Your All absolutely one hundred percent correct.
I was severely wrong when I wrote "for me
Punk Rock is dead. although it is dead
for me which were the key words I wrote
in those oh so negative and retarded linear
notes. The ~~two~~ word~~s~~ for was miss printed
at the ~~printing~~ offices when they translated
my handwriting. ~~Instead~~ The word to was
used instead of which is a very common
occurance when deadlines are due and
people are scratching like mexican fighting cocks
to get an approval for something as non important
as liner notes to a B- side cash cow.
  Yes friends. punk rock is dead for me.

Letter to the Editor.
I thought I would let the
world know how much I
Love ~~People~~. I thought
I would ~~make something art~~ try to create something that
I would personally like to listen to.
because a very large portion
of this worlds art sucks
beyond description. ~~But~~ yet I
~~Besides~~ feel that. It's a waste of
time to pass judgement. and
who the fuck am I to
declare myself an authority who's
certified, one who has the
right to critique. I guess
in a way anyone with enough
ambition to create and not
take away is someone who

233

deserves respect. There are
~~those~~ who are better at it than
others. there are some who
have severely large amounts
of enthusiasm who are prolific
as Hell, spewing out a million
products a year. Yeah products.
they are ones who usually give
10% good and 90% crap.
Then there are those who spend
years studying other peoples
works because they dont have
a chance in Hell to produce
anything with a hint of talent.
Yeah talent. But like I
said no one should be denied
the priviledge to create
and some people most

Certainly do not need the
fear of whether their goods
are better or worse
than the Best or worse.
They can find that out for
themselves.   maybe I
On second thought. ~~I thought~~
~~just tried to~~ let the world
~~would~~
know how much I love
myself.   like a hypocrite
in a hippie crypt.

    I hate myself and I
want to die
~~Please~~ Leave me alone.
        Love Kurdt

Love Child – He's So sensitive
Love Child – Diane
Calamity Jane – Car
Beatnik Termites – when she's nearby
Sun City Girls – Voice of America #1
Discharge – The more I see
Jadfair – the Crow
Jadfair – take a chance
Jadfair – I like Candy
Mazzy Star – Halah
Didjits – under the Christmas fish
Bags – Babylonian Gorgon
Bags – Survive
Bags – We will bury You
Sebadoh – Loser Core
Duh – spaghetti and red wine
TV Personalities – I know where Syd Barret lives
Axemen – Mourning of Youth

Side 2
Daniel Johnston
Continues Stories
Stinky Puffs – stinky Puffs theme
Hamburger
How You make A car
Baby A monster

Courtney, when I
say I love you I am not
ashamed, nor will anyone
ever ever come close to intimidating
persuading, etc me into thinking
otherwise. I wear you on
my sleeve. I spread you
out wide open with the wing
span of a peacock, yet
all too often with the attention
span of a bullet to the head.
I think its pathetic that the
entire world looks upon a
person with patience and a
calm demeanor as the desired
model citizen. yet theres
something to be said about
the ability to explain

ones self with a toned down,
tune deaf tone. And I will say it.
I am what
they call the boy who is
slow. how I metamorphorised
from hyperactive to cement
is for lack of a better knife
to the throat uh, annoying,
aggrevating, Confusing
as dense as cement.
Cement holds no other
minerals. you can't even find
fools gold in it. its strictly
man made and youve taught
me it's ok to be a man
and in the classic mans world
I parade you around proudly
like the ring on my finger
which holds no mineral.
    Also
         Love kurt

THE New improved revised
NIRVANA list of Albums
in which the person writing this has
been emotionally affected by . .
inspired to encapsulate what his
thoughts of a lifestyle in which he
MAY be ~~isteim~~ immersed in for
reasons of looking cool and hip.
OH and by the way maybe to introduce
these elititist obscure, treasures to the
unabashed

Elo: Electric light orchestra . The KNACK Get the
~~KNACK~~

(Gold. John?) 10CC the things we do for love.

HAll and oats. Rich Girl (wild cherry play that funky music)

Leo SAyer ?   Supertramp   EAgles: long Run
                   Breakfast in America

Pat Benatar?   Journey escape.   Reo spedwagen
Fleetwoodmack   Hi infidllity
Rumours   BAy City Rollers?

Seasons in the sun   Bugles: video   Beatles meet
Terry Jacks   Killed the Radio store   the Beatles

239

I Have been forced to become a reclusive RockStar
IE: No interviews, No radio appearances,   etc.
 due to the legions of self appointed authorities on music
whom are not musicians, who have not contributed anything
artistic to Rock and Roll besides maybe a few second rate
long winded, books on Rock and Roll and most importantly
who are ~~easily~~ the highest group of mysogynists of all
forms of expression.

I Have since the beginning of my first revelation in alternative thought
~~through~~ the introduction of New WAVE — then, Punk rock, then alternate
soundtracks of contemporary classic Rock. Never in years of my awareness
of Sexism have I seen a more radically venemous display of
Sexism in my life ~~————————~~ than in the past two
years.   For years Ive observed and noted the a culture
for any hint of Sexism and Ive found it in relatively small
doses compared to the present state of Rock and Roll.

From "Critics darlings" to Samantha fox simply because one of
the members of what used to be thought of as a band with members
Has married an established, ~~the~~ musical success determined by
the establishment of non musical music business somehing small tiny.

by this time. All conspiracy theories are very very real
with more proof than needed to be bothered with describing.
Beaurocracy exists as cancer in the simplest, most naive,
grass roots ~~corporate~~ businesses of pencil vendors, panhandling,
fenzine distribution, home baked hippie cookie sales agents,
up through the yawn! medical profession. Government related
protection agencies, Janitorial positions, and erm, entertainment
industries. Journalists will now break their own fingers after
engaging in finger printed display on their left breast in the form of
a a button   and they will bow down to let the artists critique
themselves and other artists. This is a fenzine written by
music fans. We know this to be true because they are musicians.
Can they write as well as they play? better.
what about Genres. A heavy metal musician cannot review,
A dance RnB soul group. Its that easy.

Elitism = punk rock
Capitalism =

If you were a music fan than you would contribute
to A fanzine.

You have no right to ask the question of: do you have
artistic control now that youre signed to a major -
for all Journalists are at the mercy of their editors.

Second rate 3rd degree burns

If we ever win any more awards we will have
3 impersonators come up and accept the awards
3 people who look fairly familiar to us.

VIDEO concept. milk it or scentless apprentice
  drunken fucked up me, man in a room full of
people at a party. man has gun and is stumbling
around falling down threatening to shoot.
man has wild glossy stare.

   play unplugged soon.

   release a compilation tape of favorite punk
songs with vinyl version of album

♡ Shaped box video

William and I sitting across from one another at a table (black and white) lots of Blinding Sun from the windows behind us holding hands staring into eachothers eyes. He gropes me from behind and falls dead on top of me. medical footage of sperm flowing through penis. A ghost vapor comes out of his chest and groin area and enters me Body.

during solo. Violin shots. chris as New wave keyboardist, and very quick edits of strobe light.

image of little 3 year old white arian, blonde girl in KKK outfit being led by the hand of a KKK parent

Same violet colors as in the New order video

Animation Doll footage.   Close up of lillies lyingon lighted draft Board.   footage of Anatomy models from kurts collection

244

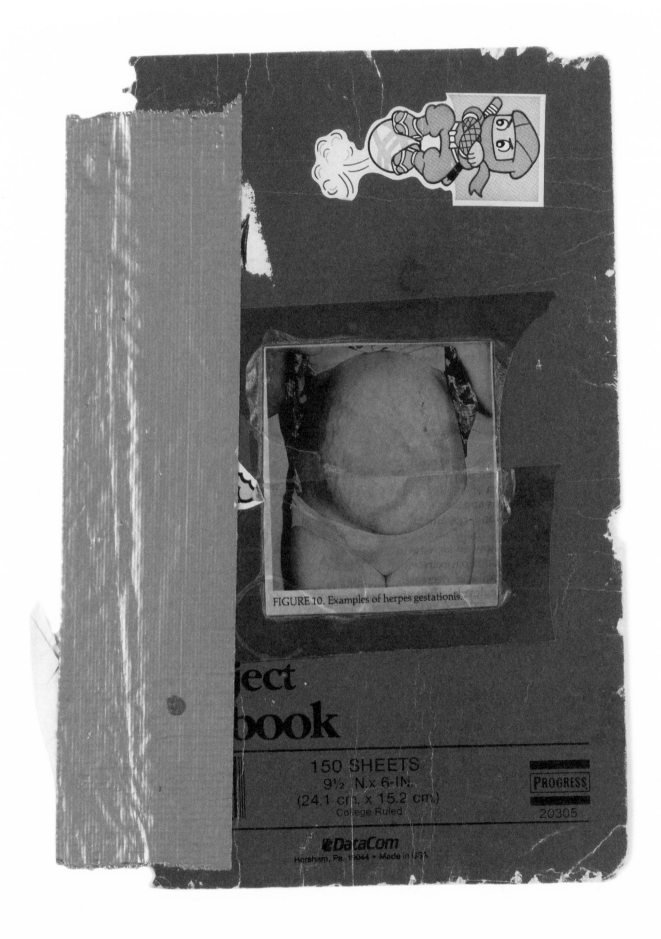

FIGURE 10. Examples of herpes gestationis.

ject
book

150 SHEETS
9½ N x 6-IN.
(24.1 cm. x 15.2 cm.)
College Ruled

PROGRESS

20305

DataCom
Horsham, Pa. 19044 • Made in USA

for many months I decided to take a break from reading rock magazines mainly to rest and clear my head from all the folk lore and current affair journalism that had been piling up since weve become a lot of peoples (dare I say) breakfast lunch and dinner gossip.

Last month I thought I'd take a peek at a few Rock mags to see whats going on and if things have cooled down.

Well, to my estimation many trees have been wasted on account of bored and boring people who still like to waste space with NIRVANA DRECK. Years ago I knew better than to believe that every article in a news paper reported everything we need to know. as in all the facts man. I knew that newspapers, magazines and history books left out things or embelished based on the special interests of the political and moral beliefs of the share holders or owners of all printed matter. Do you think a History book from the South has basically the same information on the civil war as a history book printed for the northern school districts? Do you think A right wing, Christian owned news paper reports the same as mother Jones magazine? well the rock world is a bit more confusing. Its not as cut and dry as the above refferences. People who write for music mags are a collective bunch who are at conflict every day.

As youve heard this cliché many times before music journalists are people who are paid to find as many interesting anectdotes of a musicians personality, and if there isnt enough they must spice it up and if it isn't still spicy enough which is almost always the case then, In steps the editor. an editors job is not to correct grammatical errors. his or her job is to sell magazines and to sell magazines you need to have a cupboard full of spices. So once again a journalist is almost always at the mercy of the editor. ironically journalists are the ones who obsessively try to prove that the musician has no control over their own creativity and is dictated by their record company. and the biggest and most overly used cliche of the journalist although is too true to ignore is the fact that most journalists have no idea of what its like to write a song, play an instrument or know what its like to perform on stage in front of people.

The choice to become a music journalist is usually after ones realization that they are musically retarded. but theyve worked at tower Records and own a lot of cds and rock biographies.

I found at an early age that the same people who share the same truth-witheld due to special interests conspiracy theory are usually the same people who are fans of politically motivated or music that leans towards elements of outspoken truths. PUNK ROCK. for the most part falls under this category. Quite a few years ago I felt that most of these people who listened to punk rock were aware of Commercial Rock mag sensationalism and knew better than to believe what was written in these magazines which have always ignored underground or punk Rock bands because Punk Rock doesnt sell magazines, until now. 'just like new wave. Punk rock has been cristened a new name by commercial magazines " Alternative music" And just like New WAVE only the most commercial bands are featured in these magazines.

The easiest way to advert from the chance of misrepresentation is to use the Queston Answer format. it has been proven for years that this is a safe and effective way to report the truth as long as all of the answers are printed in their entirety. When chris said "most Heavy metal kids are dumb" that was printed. What wasn't printed was the rest of it which was," and I was one of those dumb Heavy metal kids. Its not their fault because there are stupid Heavy metal bands carrying on the legacy of sexism and homophobia in white boy rock and roll." The most interesting thing about our supposed contradictory attitudes and statements made almost 2 years ago is that all of those interviews were conducted within a span of 2 to 3 months and anyone given the surprise of becoming instant rock stars against their will have the same thoughts running through their heads. Basically what we felt was a danger. the threat of losing contact with the very people whom we felt shared the same commercial/corporate magazine conspiracy theory as we did. But as it turns out pages and pages of letters bitching about our negative reactions (which were nothing more then precautionary) littered every fanzine this side of the world.

In conclusion those same people who we felt an honest love and mutual bond with bought the current affair hype hook line and sinker. which has left us feeling, betrayed. we simply wanted to give those dumb heavy metal kids (the kids who we used to be) an introduction to A different way of thinking and some 15 years worth of emotionally and socially important music and all we got was flack, backstabbing and pearl Jam.

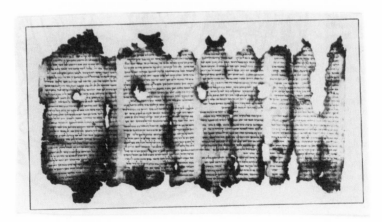

whithin the months between october 1991 thru december 92
I have had 4four Notebooks filled with two years worth of
poetry and personal writings and thoughts Lyrics stolen from
me at seperate times. two 90 minute cassettes filled
with new guitar and singing parts for new songs damaged
from a plumbing accident, as well as two of my most
expensive, favorite guitars . I've never been a very prolific
person so when creativity flows, it flows. I find myself
scribbling on little note pads and pieces of loose paper which
results in a very small portion of my writings to ever show
up in true form. Its my fault but the most violating
thing ive felt this year is not the media exxagerations
or the catty gossip, but the rape of my personal
thoughts. ripped out of pages from my stay in hospitals
and aeroplane rides hotel stays etc. I feel compelled
to say fuck you Fuck you to those of
you who have absolutely no regard for me as a person.
You have raped me harder than you'll ever know, so again
I say fuck you although this phrase has totally
lost its meaning   FUCK YOU !

FUCK you.

Sore bahrre astray the Gouna hs been found dead in a
He Shouldnt A been bed :

Dead and blasted fed and bearded poet.

~~Oqui is on plde the the Republican considered in that word~~

90% of the adult American population were not
concerned with nor had any desire to see or hear
about woodstock. 90% of the woodstock Generation are
not old Hippies now with children and the priviledge of
infusing their once young liberal ideals into the new society
in which they now are responsible for

Yes, Every one of our parents likes to hear the same old
NO 1 Hits of the 60's & 70 and lead us to believe that
they were active in the revolutionary methods of thinking
and Idealtic ubrence of naivety they just couldnt wait
to open up and use once thy got into power
the majority were then ~~best~~ a product of fetal inflation
produced by the fear and shock of the world war.
They took the bait, stayed in their classes, remembered
the scriptures of Donna Reid, graduated from High School and
had children. The Hippies are the baby boomers younger
Brothers and sisters and the Hippies were a very small breed
of veal who never managed to teach the basics to theirs
and their older brothers and sisters that of peace, love, restim nation

Hippies when I was a child. by the way my generation is the children of the
~~older~~ brothers and sisters we who in order of keeping the tradition of rebellion
get Republican tattoos on our asses ~~to spite our folts~~ and dont take a damn thing seriously
do spite our filthy hippie parents. and these & sad pathetic sensitive types who carry
the tragic burden of taking everything too serious and making everyone feel uncomfortable
I remember thinking all hippies were evil baby **killers** like charles Manson.
I only remember a few things about Jimmy Carter, He had big lips
and licked peanuts. I know now that Jimmy Carter was and is a good man
Jimmy Carter is a good, honest, smart man.

Eric Clapton dusty Blues riffs

Hi, I played the snare drum in school band from ~~the fifth~~ grades five to ~~eleven through~~ nine. during this time I didn't bother learning how to ~~actually~~ read sheet music, I just ~~waited~~ waited ~~waited for~~ for the geek in first chair to ~~play~~ learn ~~to play the~~ each song, ~~and~~ then I simply copied him, I ~~got~~ managed

to do well By ~~just fine~~ without ever having ~~to ever~~ ~~learned~~ how to read music. It took me 5 years to realize ~~the~~ ~~How~~ rhythmically retarded I was as a drummer, so I sold some of my fathers guns ~~then~~ used the money to purchase my first six string electric guitar. ~~I took one week of lessons~~

I learned everything I needed to ~~know~~ from one week of lessons which ~~are~~ resulted in the famous ~~I learned the~~ louie louie chords.

musical knowledge of E A B

weird Al

I noticed that
~~then I~~ ~~you can~~ I could use the finger positions from
the B note anywhere on the guitar, this is
known as the power chord. ; ~~that~~
~~There I started writing my~~
And so after figuring out songs like
Kingsmen Jouie Jouie travis wild thing, and crs. my best friends girl
I decided that in order to become a big famous
Rock star I would need to ~~start~~ write my
very OWN songs instead of wasting my
time learning other peoples because if you ~~do~~
Obstruct ~~just~~ study other peoples music too much It
may ~~keep~~ ~~you~~ Act as an obstruction ~~from~~ IN developing you
your very own personal ~~style~~ ~~which~~ ~~I~~ ~~al~~ style
    Someone told me that there are All across the overworld
~~the~~ Guitar institutes of technology ~~throughout our~~
Great land. where they teach you how to be
A lame un-original jukebox heroe
with stars in ~~your~~ eyes
    your

    Uh, Gee I guess what im trying to say
is: theory is a waste of time
Dorian modes are ~~for~~ ~~dicks~~ ~~losers~~ technically anal Boys with Bad values
make up your own music.
    Eric Clapton plays second rate dusty blues licks.
  ; Too much practice is like too much sugar.
    weird Al Yankovic is Americas modern pop-Rock Genious
    Do your own thing ~~not~~ others ~~there~~ ~~is~~ own their own thing.
If you copy too much ~~or~~ You'll find yourself in late night
    cocktail lounge cover band limbo.
  PS: ; the guitar part ~~to~~ for
    come as you are is the same as a song called
    the "eighties by killing Joke and
    Teen spirit has an uncanny resemblance to Godzilla
        by Blue Oyster Cult and the culture AC/DC

The Guitar has twelve notes
The Guitar is based on mathematics

Guitar
oriented   ~~who plays~~ Rock and Roll has been Around
for over 30 years ~~and~~ when ~~your~~ working
                the structure
within ~~the~~ ofA standard 4/4 Rock ~~time signature~~ rhythm ~~structure~~
                Consider
~~their limitations~~ So ~~think~~ this music
      Are
book As something just to
own like ~~a~~ A bottle cap collection
                    Family
or Baseball cards or A photo album
or an example of just exactly how
not to brighten your musical capabilities—
              Happy motoring
              love kurt

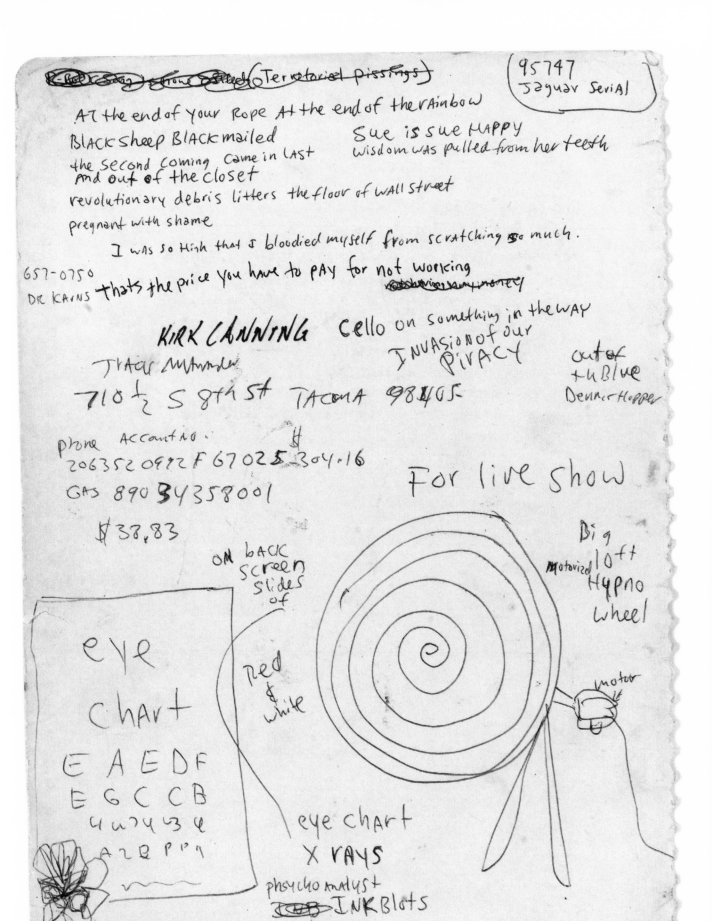

~~Rape Me~~ ~~Stone Steel~~ (Territorial Pissings)

95747
Jaguar Serial

At the end of Your Rope At the end of the rainbow
Black sheep Black mailed   Sue is sue HAPPY
the second Coming came in Last   wisdom was pulled from her teeth
and out of the closet
revolutionary debris litters the floor of Wall street
pregnant with shame
    I was so high that I bloodied myself from scratching so much.
657-0750
Dr Kairns Thats the price you have to pay for not working ~~~~

KIRK CANNING   Cello on something in the WAY
                    INVASION of our
                         PIVACY   out of
    ~~Trans Ampndr~~   the Blue
    710½ S 8th St TACOMA 98405   Dennis Hopper

phone Account No:
206 352 0922 F 67025 304.16
GAS 890 34 358 001

$38.83

                                    For live show
        on back
        screen   Big
        slides   Motorized loft
        of   Hypno
eye   wheel
                red &
chart   white
E A E D F   motor
E G C C B
4 w 3 4 3 e
A 2 e P P q   eye chart
                X rays
                phsycho analyst
                ~~~~ INK Blots

Hope I die before I turn into Pete Townshend.

At this point in our uh, career, before ~~eyesine~~ hair loss treatment ~~and Jackson Browne~~ and bad credit. ~~Iwe~~ I've decided that ~~I some~~ have no desire to do an interview with Rolling Stone. We couldn't benefit from it because the Average Rolling Stone reader is a middle aged ex hippie — turned hippiecrite who embraces the past as "the glory days," ~~and claims to~~ has and a kinder, gentler, more adult approach ~~towards~~ towards liberal conservatism. The average Rolling Stone reader ~~is a middle aged adult~~ has always ~~been aware of~~ Denied the underworlds musical options ~~and have denied this~~ unless it becomes an obviously safe ~~was~~ commodity.

I've always felt it was kind of necessary to help out the "now Generation" internally destroy the enemy ~~by~~ by posing as or using the enemy. but the now generation doesn't read Rolling Stone, so we'll jest sit ~~around~~ and wait until the old school starves like dinosaurs while the diaper school begins to litter the floors of wall street with "Real love" — revolutionary debris. Smells like thirty something.

I would only wear a tie dyed T shirt if it were ~~made from~~ dyed with the urine of Phil Collins and the blood of Gerry Garcia.

Ideas:

Buy a really powerful Ham radio system connected to A satellite dish ~~☐~~ in order to listen to any college rock station in da country. <u>note</u> House for sale with weeping willow has one in its attic. check into it! per Joan of Landmark realty

TOP 50 by NIRVANA

Raw power
Stooges

Surfer Rosa
Pixies

POD
Breeders

Pink EP
Vaselines

Philosophy of the World
Shaggs

Land shark
Fang

millions of Dead Cops
M.D.C

1st EP
scratch acid

1st EP
saccharin Trust

Pee Pee the Sailor
Butthole Surfers

My War
Black flag

Rock for light
Bad Brains

Entertainment
Gang of four

Nevermind the Bollocks
sex pistols

Its only Right and natural
Frogs

Dry
P.J. Harvey

Daydream Nation
Sonic Youth

Get the knack
the knack

Know your product
the Saints

anything by:
Kleenex

Raincoats LP
Raincoats

Colossal youth
Young marble Giants

Rocks
Acrosmith

what is this?
Punk comp California

Green
R.E.M

Burning farm cassette
Shonen Knife

typical Girls
slits

Combat Rock
Clash

Void/Faith EP
void/Faith

Rites of spring
Rites of spring

Jamboree
Beat Happening

tales of terror
tales of terror

last sessions Vol 1
Leadbelly

Superfuzz Bigmuff
mudhoney

Yip jump music
Daniel Johnston

Generic Flipper
Flipper

meet the Beatles
Beatles

we are those who ache with amorous love
Half Japanese

Locust abortion technician
Butthole Surfers

Damaged
Black Flag

the Record
Fear

Flowers of Romance
PIL

Takes a nation of millions
Public Enemy

Beach Party
marine Girls

the man who Sold the world
David Bowie

Is this real?
Wipers

Youth of America
wipers

Over the edge
Wipers

Mazzy star
Mazzy star

Raping a slave
Swans

257

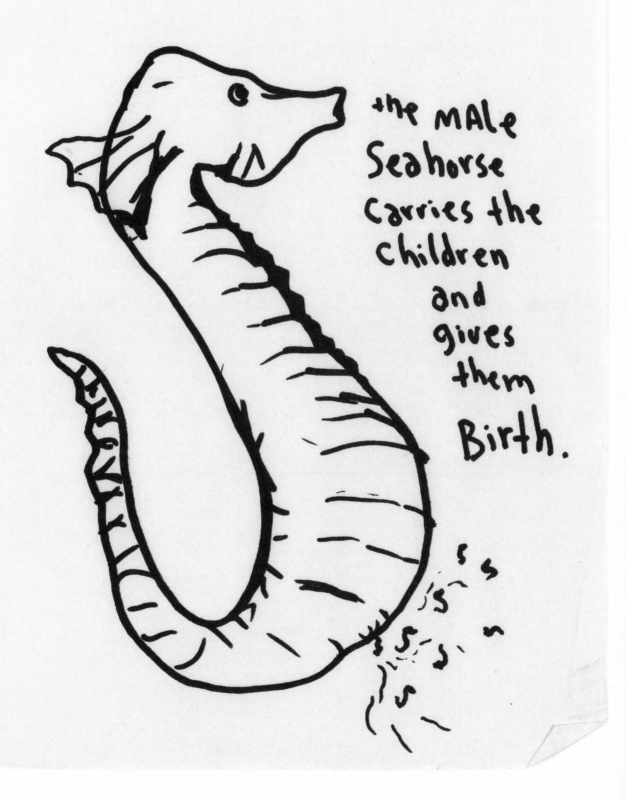

the MALe
Seahorse
Carries the
Children
and
gives
them
Birth.

when I think of Right wing I think of Ronald Reagan Clones as mayor in every state of the US.

When I hear the term Right wing I think of Hitler and Satan and Civil war. When I think of Right wingers I think of terrorists ~~and~~ who plot to kill and terrorize the lives of planned parenthood practionists. The reality of actually getting an abortion in this country is very scarce right now due to Randell Terry and his pro life gestapo who gather in churches dressed in the best camouflage ~~possible~~ (~~middle~~ lower-middle-class cameleon polyester from the wrack-es of the home shopping network. IN the house of god, Operation Rescue, (Ter... pet nonprofit organization) plot to unveil yet another helpful house hold hint to helping their duty as god fearing common folk. They either break into or enter during business hours posing as ~~patients at~~ abortion clinics and set off   bombs which release a   gas that will absorb into every inch of the clinic ruining every single instrument within that clinic. They put nails in the driveways of clinic staff and doctors. ~~they~~ make never ending threatening and violently abusive phone calls. ~~to clinic staff and doctors~~ They stand outside abortion clinics every day all day with pickets and loud, violent and threatening words of wisdom from GOD. to anyone within miles often ~~of~~ physically stopping patients from entering. Yes these people have criminal records, they have marksman ~~skills~~ and terrorist skills. They are way ahead of the game than their enemy. They steal fetuses from abortion clinic dumpsters and disposal receptions and pass sometimes, hundreds of ~~several~~ mutilated fetuses between households to be stored in boxes or zip loc baggies in freezers and in the family garage. The ~~fetuses~~ rotting deteriorating fetuses are then thrown at senators congressmen or just about anyone involved in government who is a ~~Democrat~~. These people who are terrorists are also people who have basically the same beliefs as white supremists who also claim to act and embrace their ideals on the grounds of GAWD.
They post names addresses and phone numbers of patients scheduled to have abortions and the doctors to be performing the operation. They have a computer network of information available everywhere in the united states. Right wing is the foulest, dirtiest, insult a person could be called. These people hate minorities of all color, they will perform mass extermination of everything that is not white, ~~and~~ god fearing and Right wing R is for Republican.
Right now in the state of Florida there are no available abortion doctors or
     clinics to be serviced by.   Ethnic cleansing is going on right now in the inner citys of the united states. Blacks, hispanicks and others are being exterminated before they can reach the fifth grade. The Right wing republicans ~~have been~~ Are responsible for releasing, crack and Aids in our inner citys. Their logic is ~~better~~ kill living breathing, free-thinking humans rather than unknowing unstimulated, growing cells, Encased in A lukewarm chamber.

Cartoons, Saxophones and jazz Drumming
do not mix with rock and roll

Cermudgeon

pissy little
self appointed
Judge-curmudgeon
Oh the Guilt!
the Guilt!
the autographs
the fame
the lights
the flash
the glitter
the Guilt
the Guilt

I can't sing
or
play
or
rhyme,
I think that's
Just fine

Individual
T shirts

Kurt Don
CoBain

Hair:
whatever
eyes: closed
Mouth: smaller
than Chris's
weight:
Borderline
Anorexic

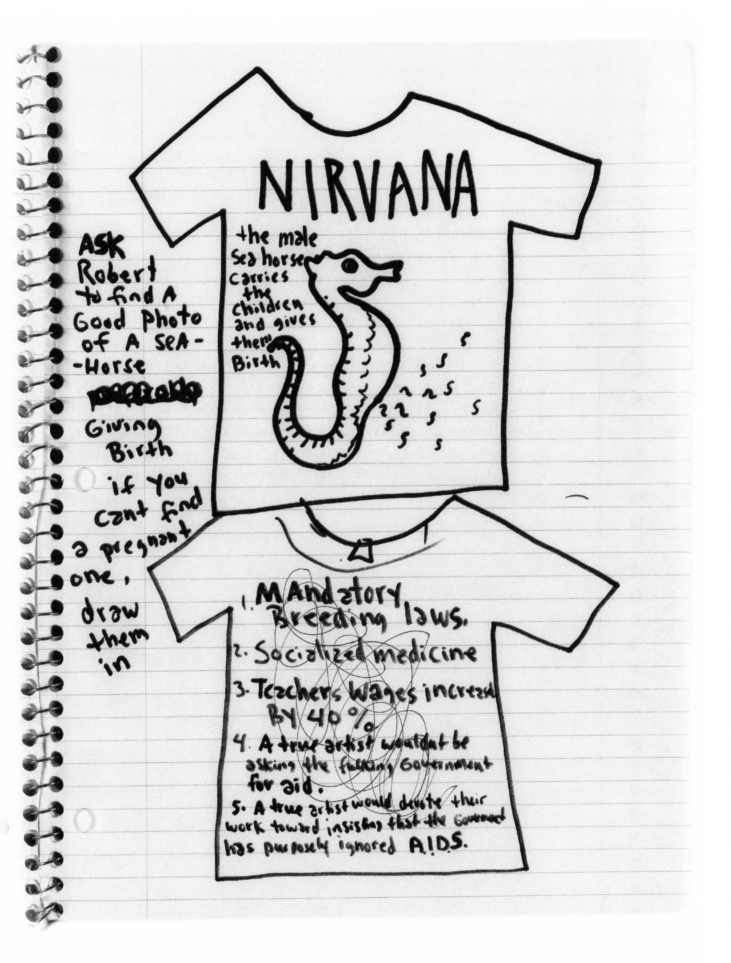

NIRVANA

ASK Robert to find A Good photo of A SEA- -Horse ~~pregnant~~ Giving Birth if you cant find a pregnant one, draw them in

the male Sea horse Carries the Children and gives them Birth

1. MAndatory Breeding laws.
2. Socialized medicine
3. Teachers wages increased BY 40%
4. A true artist wouldnt be asking the fucking Government for aid.
5. A true artist would devote their work toward insisting that the Government has purposely ignored A.!D.S.

for Boys

step # one: ~~make me a sandwich~~

remember that your older brothers cousins, uncles, and
your fathers are not your role models. this means
you do not do what they do, you do not do what they say.
They come from a time when their role models told their
sons to be mean to girls, to think of yourself as better
and stronger and smarter than them. They also taught things
like; you will grow up strong if you act tough and
fight the boys who are known as nerds or Geeks,

~~and smaller weak looking boys who come from~~
~~families who don't have enough money or the other~~
~~boys who are smart and get good grades believe their ideas~~
~~must be sissies of the lot their boys act so smart.~~

~~The early 80's saw an acceptance of the counterculture~~

The early 80's saw the white-male-corporate oppressors
acceptance ~~to wit of the~~ of A new musical counterculture ~~with~~ stemmed from the birth
of Punk Rock. Well, the clash, the sex pistols
and even the melodic accessability of the
Ramones didn't break through into the mainstream.
~~Its fourteen years to~~
~~Its fourteen years later.~~
The result of the major labels involvement
ended with ex-punk bands ~~&~~ compromising to
such ~~extremes~~ that the only true successes
were, gasp! Billy Idol or KAYA goo-goo-

Its fourteen years later and they're at it again.
So called "Alternative" bands are being signed
left and right and the ones with more of an
edge towards compromise or mainstream are the
ones who will be successful.

NIRVANA will put out a couple of more brilliant
albums on their own terms and then become
~~so~~ frustrated with ~~so~~ being so close to general
public acceptance ~~and~~ and so ~~in debt~~ financially
in debt, that they will eventually result in releasing
spineless dance music like Gang of four.

Rape me

treatment

Black & white film

Hi steve

IN the simplest terms, here it is: . . . .

Go to one or more penitentiarys
and shoot ~~this~~ movie film portraits
of the most ugly, hardened criminals
available. preferably bald, big,
hairy and tatooed. film at least
20 or more of these fine young bucks
Sitting in their cells and at the
visiting booths and tables. from the
SKinny chest up. we need at least 5 to 10
male Bitches with thick eyeshadow ~~and~~ and
their denim jail shirt sleeves rolledup
to ~~~~ the bottom half of their shirt
tied up exposing thir Stomachs

during the lines "my favorite inside source
ill Kiss your open sores appreciate your concern you
Gonna stink and burn"   we need footage of
a Chaotic press scene with lots of reporters with
more cameras and photo flashes ~~~~
out side on the steps of a court house. then a
inside the courtroom a ~~few~~

Rape me treatment   Kurdt

Black and White Portrait-footage of the men
who did the crime and are now doing time.
Big, Bald, sweaty, tattoved love boys cast
from the waist up in their cold, concrete tanks.
lounging on their bunks. striped and branded with
the shadows of prison bars across their chest, face
and walls.   We need about ten to fifteen different
characters. all 200lbs plus and also about 5 to 8 more
of whom we call the bitches: skinny, feminine,
tight pants wearin, rolled up prison shirts showing
their soft, vulnerable frames. stomaches. 150lbs and less
   There are many "Behind prison Walls," books for
refference.   whites, blacks, Italians.

Close ups of female hands lathering up soap. violent,
scrubbing hands. soapy wash cloth, begging to be clean.
starting in Black & white fading to color as the hands get cleaner.
Close ups of:
Stock footage of flowers blooming in time lapsed motion. } Color
Prefferably lillies, orchids. ya know vaginal flowers. and now
they wither and shrink up.
   Sea horses footage carousing about. floating slowly.
loving life and one another. } Color michael Meisel has found
some of this footage already.

A man lying in a gynecological chair with legs up in sturrops.

Hi fellow Advocatees,
1993 Came and went without notice.
   Besides finishing a record in which we are quite
proud of, yet getting shit from people claiming "commercial
suicide" before it's release. I must say yes, 1993 has been
a most fruitful year. Frances is a sprouting, cherubic joy
and has helped in more ways than she will ever know.
   She has helped us become more relaxed and less concerned with
those wacky Right wing ~~conspirators~~ terrorists failed attempts at

Scott

I made about 5 million dollars last year.
And I'm not giving a red cent to that elitifist
little fuck Calvin Johnson. NO WAY!
I've collaborated with one of my only Idols williamr
Burroughs and I couldn't feel cooler.
I moved away to LA for a year and came back
to find that 3 of my best friends have become
full blown heroine addicts. I've learned to hate
Riot Girl. a movement in which I was a witness
to its very initial inception because I fucked the
girl who put out the first Grrl style fanzine and
now she is exploiting the fact that she fucked
me. not in a huge way but enough to feel
exploited. but thats ok besuse I chose to
let corporate white men exploit me a few years
ago and I love it. it feels good. and I'm
not gonna donate a single dollar to the fucking
needy indie fascist regime. they can starve.
let them eat vinyl. every crumb for himself.
I'll be able to sell my untalented, very un-genius
ass for years based on my cult status.

1993 came and went without realizing it. ~~It happened~~

Besides recording a record in which we are quite proud of
and getting shit ~~for it before anyone~~ from people who havent heard it
I must say, yes it was a fruitful year. frances is a sproutly
cherubic joy and has helped in more ways then shell ever know by
helping us become more relaxed and less concerned with the foiled
attempts by the right wing conspirators and terrorists to cut off our
rightful supply of fame fortune and the american way God bless this
mess and thank god for the right to chuse ~~freedom of terror~~ USA today and
uh, kill a queer for God bumper stickers. (thanks william, for the
last remark.) yeah I got to meet and do a record with one of the
only people I admire. that was a plus, and ~~so~~ equally so was
the pleasure of doing the Advocate interview. of all the gut spilling
Ive done Ive never felt so relaxed than with _____
He was very encouraging and sympathetic. what can I say?
thank you Ill always be an Advocate for you fags. I love you.
and apreciate the gracious compliments ~~for the~~
Hey you should interview Bruce la Bruce from canada he's made
some fantastic films. Hope noone felt Ive been too patronizing ~~the others~~
~~paranoid~~   Love kurdt. stay Gay all the way and ~~they may be deprogramed~~
so ~~easy~~   wipe your Ass with USA
                                                                            today.

Kevin Allman

Scott

In movies the filmmaker tries to depict true life instances. the most interesting occurrences during the subjects time frame are picked out of a span of time. Time is much longer than a movie can show and a viewer will have the patience for. therefore we don't realize how time plays such a gigantic part in the leading up to events. two people may have dinner for 2 hours but only 30 seconds of the most interesting parts of the conversation will be used. I feel time and a persons ability to understand time is very important its the only way I can relate to you the very real way a person becomes addicted to substances If we realize and remember things happen over a period of time. then we may understand how ~~one becomes a drug addict~~ almost everyone who tries hard drugs ie: heroine and cocaine will eventually become literally, a slave to these substances.

I remember someone saying If you try heroine once you'll become hooked. of course I laughed and scoffed at the idea but I now believe this to be very true. not literally, I mean If you do dope once you dont instantly become addicted it usually takes about one month of every day use to physically become addicted. but after the first time your mind say ahh that was very pleasant as long as I dont do it every day I wont have a problem. the problem is it happens over time. lets start with January 1st lets do dope for the first time. conciously you wont do it again for maybe a month. february you'll do it twice. march 3 days in a row, february, 3 days in a row and once more at the end of the month. march, maybe not at all. april 5 days in a row skip 3 once more. may 10 days in a row. during those ten days its very easy to lose track of time it may seem like 3 days but two weeks can go by. The effects are still as pleasant and you can still choose

Hotel Villa Magna, S.A. - Inscrita en el Registro Mercantil de Madrid, Tomo 1993 General, Tomo 1381 de la Sección 3ª, Folio 1, Hoja 10.994 Insc. 1ª. 26/5/56. CIF A-28-157113

what days you do it so naturally there must not be a problem.
with everyone sometime at least once a year some sort of crisis
happens to everyone, the loss of a friend or mate or relative
this is when the drug tells you to say fuck it.
every drug addict has said fuck it more times than they
can count. This example has only taken one page but
within a year of casual heroine use the person has had
more days off dope than on. It can slowly and
gradually consume you because there are 24 hrs in a day
and no one wants to be hooked. It doesn't happen as
fast as it does in a movie because a movie quickly
has to show all the juicy stuff within 2 hrs.
2 hrs out of 2 years worth of casual drug use is
nothing. by the time youve said fuck it the
long process of trying to stay off begins.
The first kick is usually easy if you have pills.
you basically sleep. which is bad in my opinion
because you think if its that easy I could get
hooked and kick for the rest of my life.

by the second and third time it becomes
very different. It takes sometimes 5 times
longer, the psychological factors have set in
and are as damaging as the physical effects.
every time you kick as time goes by it gets
more uncomfortable, even the most needle phobic person can
crave the relief of putting a syringe in their arm. people have
been known to shoot wAter, booze, mouthwash etc...
drug use is escapism whether you want to admit it or not.
a person may have spent months, years trying to get help. but
the amount of time one spends trying to get help and the years it
takes to become completely drug free is nothing in comparison.
every junkie ive ever met has fought with it at least 5 years and
most end up fighting for about 15-25 years, until finally
they have to resort to becoming a slave to another drug the 12 step
program which is in itself another drug / religion. If it works for
you do it. If your ego is too big start at square one and
go the psychological rehabilit. way. either way youve got
at least 5 to 10 years of battle ahead of you.

HOTEL EXCELSIOR
Roma

He said, yes Larry as in Larry King
when we were shooting the film ive
found the indigenous people of ALASKA
to be some of the most warm friendly,
blah blah blah etc. Another retarded
action Adventure side of beef longing to
portray himself as a distinguished actor.
His P.R man transcribed a basic English
101 course on A piece of paper and
Jean Clod Clod goddammne actor
man must have studied the Answers
to the hallowing questions that Larry
will be asking for at lesst a week.
Now thats Entertainment! watching
Sylvester Stallone fumble his way thrugt
An interview with that yo duh

Fred Flintstone accent while spewing out
sentences that maybe uh A really smart
guy might say ya know with a lot of
as well as pertaining to. etc. blah.
 The indigenous people of ALASKA?
What are you fucking talking about?
the Eskimos? or the drunken
Redneck settlers who never see sunshine
who are up to their ball sacks with
raw dead fish guts on A boat
for 9 months out of the year.

NOTES

A note about the letters: Kurt often wrote a draft before completing the final version of a letter. Some of the letters included in this book represent those drafts, while others are letters that were never sent.

Page 1:
Letter to Dale Crover, the drummer for the Melvins, an Aberdeen rock band that heavily influenced early Nirvana.

Page 15:
Letter to Dave Foster, Nirvana's second drummer, who was fired shortly before the recording sessions for "Love Buzz."

Page 19:
Letter to Mark Lanegan, lead singer of the Seattle band Screaming Trees.

Page 30:
Letter to Jesse Reed, Kurt's best friend from high school.

Page 37:
NIRVANA
Kenichewa
Dear _____.
NIRVANA is a three piece from the outskirts of Seattle WA.
Kurdt-Guitar/Voice and Chris-bass have struggled with too many undedicated drummers for the past 3 years, per-forming under such names as: Bliss, throat Oyster, Pen Cap Ch[ew] Ted ed Fred etc . . . for the last 9 months we have had the pleasure to take Chad-drums under our wings and develop what we are now and always will be NIRVANA.
3 regularly broadcasted carts on K.C.M.U. (Seattle College Radio also KAOS Olympia)
Played with: Leaving Trains, Whipping Boy, Hells Kitchen, Trecherous Jaywalkers & countless local acts.
Looking for: EP or LP We have about 15 songs Recorded on 8 Tracks at Reciprocal Studios in Seattle.
Willing to compromise on material (some of this shit is pretty old.) Tour Any-time forever hopefully the music will speak for itself
Please Reply Thank You Area Code (206) N PEAR Olympia WA. 98506

Page 60:
Kurt's questions for a fanzine interview with the Melvins.

Page 92:

Letter to Eugene Kelly from the Vaselines, a Scottish band that was one of Kurt's favorites. Kelly later became a member of Captain America and Eugenius.

Page 134:

A list of possible producers for "Nevermind."

Pages 156-159:

Draft of record company bio of the band for "Nevermind." This bio was never used.

Page 160:

List of elements needed for "Smells Like Teen Spirit" video.

Pages 167-172:

Letter to Tobi Vail, drummer for the Olympia band Bikini Kill, written a few days after the completion of the "Nevermind" recording sessions in spring 1991.

Page 177:

Concept for "Come as You Are" video.

Pages 213-214:

Letter to Donald Cobain, Kurt's father.

Page 215:

Fax from recording engineer Steve Albini on which Kurt made notes about the recording gear to be used for "In Utero."

Page 216:

Notes for the recording of "In Utero."

Pages 219-220:

Letter to Simon Timony of the Stinky Puffs.

Page 228:

Proposed marketing plan for "In Utero."

Page 231:

Concept for "Heart-Shaped Box" video.

Page 240:

I have been forced to become a reclusive Rock Star

IE: No interviews, no radio appearances, etc. due to the legions of self appointed authorities on music who are not musicians, who have not contributed anything artistic to Rock and Roll besides maybe a few second rate long winded, books on Rock and Roll and most importantly who are the highest group of mysogynists in all forms of expression.

I have since the beginning of my first revelation in alternative thought through the introduction of New Wave— then, Punk rock, then alternative soundtracks of Contemporary Classic Rock. Never in years of my awareness of sexism have I seen a more radically venomous display of sexism in my life than in the past two years. for years I've observed and waited like a vulture for any hint of sexism and I've found it in relatively small doses compared to the present state of Rock and Roll, from critics darlings to Samantha fox simply because one of the members of what used to be thought of as a band with members Has married an established, musical, success determined by the establishment of non musical music writers. Something smells fishy!

Page 241:

by this time, All conspiracy theories are very very real. With more proof than needed to be bothered with describing. Beaurocracy exists as cancer in the simplest, most naive, grass roots business of pencil vendors, panhandling, fanzine distribution, home baked, hippie cookie sales agents up through the yawn; medical profession, Government related protection agencies, Janitorial positions, and erm, entertainment industries. Journalists will now break their own fingers after engaging in each individuals display of fingerprints on their left breast in the form of a button and they will bow down to let the artists critique themselves and other artists. This is a fanzine written by music fans. We know this to be true because they are musicians. Can they write as well as they play? better. What about Genres. A heavy metal musician cannot review, a dance RnB soul group. It's that easy.
Elitism = Punk Rock
Capitalism =

Page 242:

If you were a music fan than you would contribute to a fanzine.
You have no right to ask the question: do you have artistic control now that you've signed to a major. for all Journalists are at the mercy of their editors.
Second rate 3rd degree burns

Page 243:

If we ever win any more awards we will have 3 impersonators come up and accept the award 3 people who look fairly familiar to us.
Video Concept. Milk it or scentless apprentice drunken fucked up me, man in a room full of people at a party man has gun and is stumbling around falling down threatening to shoot.
man has wild glossy stare.
play unplugged soon.
release a compilation tape of favorite punk songs with vinyl version of album

Page 244:
❤ Shaped box video
William and I sitting across from one another at a table (Black and White) lots of Blinding Sun from the windows behind us holding hands staring into each others eyes. He gropes me from behind and falls dead on top of me. medical footage of sperm flowing through penis. A ghost vapor comes out of his chest and groin area and enters me Body.
during solo. Violin shots. Chris as New Wave keyboardist and very quick edits of strobe light.
image of little 3 year old white, arian, blonde girl in KKK outfit being led by the hand of a KKK parent
Same violet colors as in the New order video
Animation Doll footage. Close up of lillies lying on lighted draft Board. footage of Anatomy models from Kurts collection

Pages 264-265:
Concepts for "Rape Me" video that was never made.

Page 269-270:
Hotel Villa Magna
Madrid
In movies the filmmaker tries to depict true life instances, the most interesting occurances during the subjects time frame are picked out of a span of time. Time is much longer than a movie can show and a viewer will have

the patience for. therefore we don't realize how time plays such a gigantic part in the leading up to events. two people may have dinner for 2 hours but only 30 seconds of the most interesting parts of the conversation will be used. I feel time and a persons ability to understand time is very important. its the only way I can relate to you the very real way a person becomes addicted to substances If we realize and remember things happen over a period of time, then we may understand how almost everyone who tries hard drugs ie: heroine and cocaine will eventually become literally, a slave to these substances.

I remember someone saying if you try heroine once you'll become hooked. Of course I laughed and scoffed at the idea but I now believe this to be very true. Not literally, I mean if you do dope once you don't instantly become addicted it usually takes about one month of every day use to physically become addicted. but after the first time your mind say ahh that was very pleasant as long as I don't do it every day I won't have a problem. the problem is it happens over time. lets start with January 1st lets do dope for the first time. Conciously you won't do it again for maybe a month. febuary youll do it twice. march 3 days in a row. february, 3 days in a row and once more at the end of the month. march, maybe not at all. april 5 days in a row Skip 3 once more. May 10 days in a row. during those ten days it's very easy to lose track of time it may seem like 3 days but two weeks can go by. The effects are still as pleasant and you can still choose what days you do it so naturally there must not be a problem. with everyone some time at least once a year some sort of crisis happens to everyone, the loss of a friend or mate or relative this is when the drug tells you to say fuck it. every drug addict has said fuck it more times than they can count. This example has only taken one page but within a year of casual heroine use the person has had more days off dope than on. It can slowly and gradually consume you because there are 24 hrs in a day and no one wants to be hooked. It doesn't happen as fast as it does in a movie because a movie quickly has to show all the juicy stuff within 2 hrs. 2 hrs out of a years worth of casual drug use is nothing. by the time you've said fuck it the long process of trying to stay off begins. The first kick is usually easy if you have pills. You basically sleep. which is bad in my opinion because you think if its that easy I could get hooked and kick for the rest of my life. by the second and third time it becomes very different. It takes sometimes 5 times longer. the psychological factors have set in and are as damaging as the physical effects. every time you kick as time goes by it gets more uncomfortable. even the most needle phobic person can crave the relief of putting a syringe in their arm. people have been known to shoot water, booze, mouthwash etc . . . drug use is escapism whether you want to admit it or not. a person may have spent months, years trying to get help, but the amount of time one spends trying to get help and the years it takes to become completely drug free is nothing in comparison. every junkie i've ever met has fought with it at least 5 years and most end up fighting for about 15 25 years, until finally they have to resort to becoming a slave to another drug the 12 step program which is in itself another drug/religion. If it works for you do it. If your ego is too big start at square one and go the psychological rehabilitative way. either way you've got at least 5 to 10 years of battle ahead of you.

Page 271-272:
Hotel Excelsior
Roma
He said, yes Larry as in Larry King when we were shooting the film we found the indigenous people of Alaska to be some of the most warm friendly, blah blah blah etc. Another retarded action adventure side of beef longing to portray himself as a distinguished actor. His P.R. man transcribed a basic English 101 course on a piece of paper and Jean Clod goddammne actor man must have studied the Answers to the hallowing questions that Larry will be asking for at least a week. Now thats Entertainment: watching Sylvester Stallone fumble his way through an interview with that yo duh Fred Flintstone accent while spewing out sentences that may be uh a really smart guy might say ya know with a lot of as well as, pertaining to, etc. blah. The indigenous people of Alaska? What are you fucking talking about? the Eskimos? or the drunken Redneck settlers who never see sunshine who are up to their ball sacks with raw dead fish guts on a boat for 9 months out of the year.